WAR COLLECTIVISM

Power, Business, and the Intellectual Class in World War I

WAR COLLECTIVISM

Power, Business, and the Intellectual Class in World War I

Murray N. Rothbard

MISES INSTITUTE
AUBURN, ALABAMA

Ludwig von Mises Institute
518 West Magnolia Avenue
Auburn, Alabama 36832
mises.org

ISBN: 978-1-61016-250-0

TABLE OF CONTENTS

I

War Collectivism in World War I

More than any other single period, World War I was the critical watershed for the American business system. It was a "war collectivism," a totally planned economy run largely by big-business interests through the instrumentality of the central government, which served as the model, the precedent, and the inspiration for state corporate capitalism for the remainder of the twentieth century.

That inspiration and precedent emerged not only in the United States, but also in the war economies of the major combatants of World War I. War collectivism showed the big-business interests of the Western world that it was possible to shift radically from the previous, largely free-market, capitalism to a new order marked by strong government, and extensive and pervasive government intervention and planning, for the purpose of providing a network of subsidies and monopolistic privileges to business, and especially to large business, interests. In particular, the economy could be cartelized under the aegis of government, with prices raised and production fixed and restricted, in the classic pattern of monopoly; and military and other government

---

This is reprinted from *A New History of Leviathan*, Ronald Radosh and Murray N. Rothbard, eds. (New York: E.P. Dutton & Co., 1972), pp. 66–110.

contracts could be channeled into the hands of favored corporate producers. Labor, which had been becoming increasingly rambunctious, could be tamed and bridled into the service of this new, state monopoly-capitalist order, through the device of promoting a suitably cooperative trade unionism, and by bringing the willing union leaders into the planning system as junior partners.

In many ways, the new order was a striking reversion to old-fashioned mercantilism, with its aggressive imperialism and nationalism, its pervasive militarism, and its giant network of subsidies and monopolistic privileges to large business interests. In its twentieth-century form, of course, the New Mercantilism was industrial rather than mercantile, since the industrial revolution had intervened to make manufacturing and industry the dominant economic form. But there was a more significant difference in the New Mercantilism. The original mercantilism had been brutally frank in its class rule, and in its scorn for the average worker and consumer.[1] Instead, the new dispensation cloaked the new form of rule in the guise of promotion of the overall national interest, of the welfare of the workers through the new representation for labor, and of the common good of all citizens. Hence the importance, for providing a much-needed popular legitimacy and support, of the new ideology of twentieth-century liberalism, which sanctioned and glorified the new order. In contrast to the older laissez-faire liberalism of the previous century, the new liberalism gained popular sanction for the new system by proclaiming that it differed radically from the

---

[1] On the attitudes of the mercantilists toward labor, see Edgar S. Furniss, *The Position of the Laborer in a System of Nationalism* (New York: Kelley & Millman, 1957). Thus, Furniss cites the English mercantilist William Petyt, who spoke of labor as a "capital material . . . raw and undigested . . . committed into the hands of supreme authority, in whose prudence and disposition it is to improve, manage, and fashion it to more or less advantage." Furniss adds that "it is characteristic of these writers that they should be so readily disposed to trust in the wisdom of the civil power to 'improve, manage and fashion' the economic raw material of the nation" (p. 41).

old, exploitative mercantilism in its advancement of the welfare of the whole society. And in return for this ideological buttressing by the new "corporate" liberals, the new system furnished the liberals the prestige, the income, and the power that came with posts for the concrete, detailed planning of the system as well as for ideological propaganda on its behalf.

For their part, the liberal intellectuals acquired not only prestige and a modicum of power in the new order, they also achieved the satisfaction of believing that this new system of government intervention was able to transcend the weaknesses and the social conflicts that they saw in the two major alternatives: laissez-faire capitalism or proletarian, Marxian socialism. The intellectuals saw the new order as bringing harmony and cooperation to all classes on behalf of the general welfare, under the aegis of big government. In the liberal view, the new order provided a middle way, a "vital center" for the nation, as contrasted to the divisive "extremes" of left and right.

I

We have no space here to dwell on the extensive role of big business and business interests in getting the United States into World War I. The extensive economic ties of the large business community with England and France, through export orders and through loans to the Allies, especially those underwritten by the politically powerful J.P. Morgan & Co. (which also served as agent to the British and French governments), allied to the boom brought about by domestic and Allied military orders, all played a leading role in bringing the United States into the war. Furthermore, virtually the entire Eastern business community supported the drive toward war.[2]

---

[2] On the role of the House of Morgan, and other economic ties with the Allies in leading to the American entry into the war, see Charles Callan Tansill, America Goes to War (Boston: Little, Brown & Co., 1938), pp. 32–134.

> Apart from the role of big business in pushing America down the road to war, business was equally enthusiastic about the extensive planning and economic mobilization that the war would clearly entail. Thus, an early enthusiast for war mobilization was the United States Chamber of Commerce, which had been a leading champion of industrial cartelization under the aegis of the federal government since its formation in 1912. The Chamber's monthly, *The Nation's Business*, foresaw in mid-1916 that a mobilized economy would bring about a sharing of power and responsibility between government and business. And the chairman of the U.S. Chamber's Executive Committee on National Defense wrote to the du Ponts, at the end of 1916, of his expectation that "this munitions question would seem to be the greatest opportunity to foster the new spirit" of cooperation between government and industry.[3]

The first organization to move toward economic mobilization for war was the Committee on Industrial Preparedness, which in 1916 grew out of the Industrial Preparedness Committee of the Naval Consulting Board, a committee of industrial consultants to the Navy dedicated to considering the ramifications of an expanding American Navy. Characteristically, the new CIP was a closely blended public-private organization, officially an arm of the federal government but financed solely by private contributions. Moreover, the industrialist members of the committee, working patriotically without fee, were thereby able to retain their private positions and incomes. Chairman of the CIP, and a dedicated enthusiast for industrial mobilization, was Howard E. Coffin, vice-president of the important Hudson Motor Co. of Detroit. Under Coffin's direction, the CIP organized a national inventory of thousands of industrial

---

[3] Quoted in Paul A.C. Koistinen, "The 'Industrial-Military Complex' in Historical Perspective: World War I," *Business History Review* (Winter, 1967): 381.

facilities for munitions-making. To propagandize for this effort, christened "industrial preparedness," Coffin was able to mobilize the American Press Association, the Associated Advertising Clubs of the World, the august *New York Times*, and the great bulk of American industry.[4]

The CIP was succeeded, in late 1916, by the fully governmental Council of National Defense, whose Advisory Commission—largely consisting of private industrialists—was to become its actual operating agency. (The Council proper consisted of several members of the Cabinet.) President Wilson announced the purpose of the CND as organizing "the whole industrial mechanism . . . in the most effective way." Wilson found the Council particularly valuable because it "opens up a new and direct channel of communication and cooperation between business and scientific men and all departments of the Government. . . ."[5] He also hailed the personnel of the Council's Advisory Commission as marking "the entrance of the nonpartisan engineer and professional man into American governmental affairs" on an unprecedented scale. These members, declared the President grandiloquently, were to serve without

---

[4] The leading historian of World War I mobilization of industry, himself a leading participant and director of the Council of National Defense, writes with scorn that the scattered exceptions to the chorus of business approval "revealed a considerable lack . . . of that unity of will to serve the Nation that was essential to the fusing of the fagots of individualism into the unbreakable bundle of national unity." Grosvenor B. Clarkson, *Industrial America in the World War* (Boston: Houghton Muffin, 1923), p. 13. Clarkson's book, incidentally, was subsidized by Bernard Baruch, the head of industrial war collectivism; the manuscript was checked carefully by one of Baruch's top aides. Clarkson, a public relations man and advertising executive, had begun his effort by directing publicity for Coffin's industrial preparedness campaign in 1916. See Robert D. Cuff, "Bernard Baruch: Symbol and Myth in Industrial Mobilization," *Business History Review* (Summer, 1969): 116.

[5] Clarkson, *Industrial America in the World War*, p. 21.

pay, "efficiency being their sole object and Americanism their only motive."[6]

Exulting over the new CND, Howard Coffin wrote to the du Ponts in December, 1916, that "it is our hope that we may lay the foundation for that closely knit structure, industrial, civil and military, which every thinking American has come to realize is vital to the future life of this country, in peace and in commerce, no less than in possible war."[7]

Particularly influential in establishing the CND was Secretary of the Treasury William Gibbs McAdoo, son-in-law of the President, and formerly promoter of the Hudson and Manhattan Railroad and associate of the Ryan interests in Wall Street.[8] Head of the Advisory Commission was Walter S. Gifford, who had been one of the leaders of the Coffin Committee and had come to government from his post as chief statistician of the American Telephone and Telegraph Co., a giant monopoly enterprise in the Morgan ambit. The other "nonpartisan" members were: Daniel Willard, president of the Baltimore and Ohio Railroad; Wall Street financier Bernard M. Baruch; Howard E. Coffin; Julius Rosenwald, president of Sears, Roebuck and Co.; Samuel Gompers, president of the AF of L; and one scientist and one leading surgeon.

---

[6] Ibid., p. 22.

[7] Koistinen, "The 'Industrial-Military Complex' in Historical Perspective: World War I," p. 385.

[8] Originating the idea of the CND was Dr. Hollis Godfrey, president of the Drexel Institute, an industrial training and management education organization. Also influential in establishing the CND was the joint military-civilian Kerner Board, headed by Colonel Francis J. Kerner, and including as its civilian members: Benedict Crowell, chairman of Crowell & Little Construction Co. of Cleveland and later Assistant Secretary of War; and R. Goodwyn Rhett, president of the People's Bank of Charleston, and president as well of the Chamber of Commerce of the United States. Koistinen, "The 'Industrial-Military Complex' in Historical Perspective: World War I," pp. 382, 384.

Months before American entry into the war, the Advisory Commission of the CND designed what was to become the entire system of purchasing war supplies, the system of food control, and censorship of the press. It was the Advisory Commission that met with the delighted representatives of the various branches of industry, and told the businessmen to form themselves into committees for sale of their products to the government, and for the fixing of the prices of these products. Daniel Willard was, unsurprisingly, put in charge of dealing with the railroads, Howard Coffin with munitions and manufacturing, Bernard Baruch with raw materials and minerals, Julius Rosenwald with supplies, and Samuel Gompers with labor. The idea of establishing committees of the various industries, "to get their resources together," began with Bernard Baruch. CND commodity committees, in their turn, invariably consisted of the leading industrialists in each field; these committees would then negotiate with the committees appointed by industry.[9]

At the recommendation of the Advisory Commission, Herbert Clark Hoover was named head of the new Food Administration. By the end of March, 1917, the CND appointed a Purchasing Board to coordinate government's purchases from industry. Chairman of this Board, the name of which was soon changed to the General Munitions Board, was Frank A. Scott, a well-known Cleveland manufacturer, and president of Warner & Swasey Co.

---

[9] As one of many examples, the CND's "Cooperative Committee on Copper" consisted of: the president of Anaconda Copper, the president of Calumet and Hecla Mining, the vice-president of Phelps Dodge, the vice-president of Kennecott Mines, the president of Utah Copper, the president of United Verde Copper, and Murray M. Guggenheim of the powerful Guggenheim family interests. And the American Iron and Steel Institute furnished the representatives of that industry. Clarkson, *Industrial America in the World War*, pp. 496–97; Koistinen, "The 'Industrial-Military Complex' in Historical Perspective: World War I," p. 386.

Yet centralized mobilization was proceeding but slowly through the tangle of bureaucracy, and the United States Chamber of Commerce urged Congress that the director of the CND "should be given power and authority in the economic field analogous to that of the chief of state in the military field."[10] Finally, in early July, the raw materials, munitions, and supplies departments were brought together under a new War Industries Board, with Scott as Chairman, the board that was to become the central agency for collectivism in World War I. The functions of the WIB soon became the coordinating of purchases, the allocation of commodities, and the fixing of prices and priorities in production.

Administrative problems beset the WIB, however, and a satisfactory "autocrat" was sought to rule the entire economy as chairman of the new organization. The willing autocrat was finally discovered in the person of Bernard Baruch in early March, 1918. With the selection of Baruch, urged strongly upon President Wilson by Secretary McAdoo, war collectivism had achieved its final form.[11] Baruch's credentials for the task were unimpeachable; an early supporter of the drive toward war, Baruch had presented a scheme for industrial war mobilization to President Wilson as early as 1915.

The WIB developed a vast apparatus that connected to the specific industries through commodity divisions largely staffed by the industries themselves. The historian of the WIB, himself one of its leaders, exulted that the WIB had established

> a system of concentration of commerce, industry, and all the powers of government that was without compare among all the other nations. . . . It was so interwoven with the supply departments of the army and navy, of

---

[10] Clarkson, *Industrial America in the World War,* p. 28.

[11] Scott and Willard had successively been Chairman, which post was then offered to Homer Ferguson, president of the Newport News Shipbuilding Co. and later head of the United States Chamber of Commerce.

> the Allies, and with other departments of the Government that, while it was an entity of its own . . . its decisions and its acts . . . were always based on a conspectus of the whole situation. At the same time, through the commodity divisions and sections in contact with responsible committees of the commodities dealt with, the War Industries Board extended its antennae into the innermost recesses of industry. Never before was there such a focusing of knowledge of the vast field of American industry, commerce, and transportation. Never was there such an approach to omniscience in the business affairs of a continent.[12]

Big-business leaders permeated the WIB structure from the board itself down to the commodity sections. Thus, Vice-Chairman Alexander Legge came from International Harvester Co.; businessman Robert S. Brookings was the major force in insisting on price-fixing; George N. Peek, in charge of finished products, had been vice-president of Deere & Co., a leading farm equipment manufacturer. Robert S. Lovett, in charge of priorities, was chairman of the board of Union Pacific Railroad, and J. Leonard Replogle, Steel Administrator, had been president of the American Vanadium Co. Outside of the direct WIB structure, Daniel Willard of the Baltimore & Ohio was in charge of the nation's railroads, and big businessman Herbert C. Hoover was the "Food Czar."

In the granting of war contracts, there was no nonsense about competitive bidding. Competition in efficiency and cost was brushed aside, and the industry-dominated WIB handed out contracts as it saw fit.

Any maverick individualistic firm that disliked the mandates and orders of the WIB was soon crushed between the coercion wielded by government and the collaborating opprobrium of

---

[12] Clarkson, *Industrial America in the World War*, p. 63.

his organized business colleagues. Thus, Grosvenor Clarkson writes:

> Individualistic American industrialists were aghast when they realized that industry had been drafted, much as manpower had been. . . . Business willed its own domination, forged its bonds, and policed its own subjection. There were bitter and stormy protests here and there, especially from those industries that were curtailed or suspended. . . . [But] the rents in the garment of authority were amply filled by the docile and cooperative spirit of industry. The occasional obstructor fled from the mandates of the Board only to find himself ostracized by his fellows in industry.[13]

One of the most important instrumentalities of wartime collectivism was the Conservation Division of the WIB, an agency again consisting largely of leaders in manufacturing. The Conservation Division had begun as the Commercial Economy Board of the CND, the brainchild of its first chairman, Chicago businessman A.W. Shaw. The Board, or Division, would suggest industrial economies, and encourage the industry concerned to establish cooperative regulations. The Board's regulations were supposedly "voluntary," a voluntarism enforced by "the compulsion of trade opinion—which automatically policed the observance of the recommendations." For "a practice adopted by the overwhelming consent and even insistence of . . . [a man's] fellows, especially when it bears the label of patriotic service in a time of emergency, is not lightly to be disregarded."[14]

In this way, in the name of wartime "conservation," the Conservation Division set out to rationalize, standardize, and cartelize industry in a way that would, hopefully, continue

---

[13] Ibid., pp. 154, 159.

[14] Ibid., pp. 215.

permanently after the end of the war. Arch W. Shaw summed up the Division's task as follows: to drastically reduce the number of styles, sizes, etc., of the products of industry; to eliminate various styles and varieties; to standardize sizes and measures. That this ruthless and thoroughgoing suppression of competition in industry was not thought of as a purely wartime measure is made clear in this passage by Grosvenor Clarkson:

> The World War was a wonderful school. . . . It showed us how so many things may be bettered that we are at a loss where to begin with permanent utilization of what we know The Conservation Division alone showed that merely to strip from trade and industry the lumber of futile custom and the encrustation of useless variety would return a good dividend on the world's capital. . . . It is, perhaps, too much to hope that there will be any general gain in time of peace from the triumphant experiment of the Conservation Division. Yet now the world needs to economize as much as in war.[15]

Looking forward to future cartelization, Clarkson declared that such peacetime "economizing . . . implies such a close and sympathetic affiliation of competitive industries as is hardly possible under the decentralization of business that is compelled by our antitrust statutes."

Bernard Baruch's biographer summarized the lasting results of the compulsory "conservation" and standardization as follows:

> Wartime conservation had reduced styles, varieties, and colors of clothing. It had standardized sizes. . . . It had outlawed 250 different types of plow models in the U.S., to say nothing of 755 types of drills . . . mass production and mass distribution had become the law of the land. . . . This, then, would be the goal of the next quarter of the twentieth century: "To Standardize

[15] Ibid., pp. 230.

> American Industry"; to make of wartime necessity a matter of peacetime advantage.[16]

Not only the Conservation Division, but the entire structure of wartime collectivism and cartelization constituted a vision to business and government of a future peacetime economy. As Clarkson frankly put it:

> It is little wonder that the men who dealt with the industries of a nation . . . meditated with a sort of intellectual contempt on the huge hit-and-miss confusion of peacetime industry, with its perpetual cycle of surfeit and dearth and its internal attempt at adjustment after the event. From their meditations arose dreams of an ordered economic world.
>
> They conceived of America as "commodity sectioned" for the control of world trade. They beheld the whole trade of the world carefully computed and registered in Washington, requirements noted, American resources on call, the faucets opened or closed according to the circumstances. In a word, a national mind and will confronting international trade and keeping its own house in business order.[17]

Heart and soul of the mechanism of control of industry by the WIB were its sixty-odd commodity sections, committees supervising the various groups of commodities, which were staffed almost exclusively by businessmen from the respective industries. Furthermore, these committees dealt with over three hundred "war service committees" of industry appointed by the respective industrial groupings under the aegis of the Chamber of Commerce of the United States. It is no wonder that in this cozy atmosphere, there was a great deal of harmony between business and government. As Clarkson admiringly described it:

---

[16] Margaret L. Coit, *Mr. Baruch* (Boston: Houghton Muffin Co., 1957), p. 219.

[17] Clarkson, *Industrial America in the World War*, p. 312.

> Businessmen wholly consecrated to government service, but full of understanding of the problems of industry, now faced businessmen wholly representative of industry . . . but sympathetic with the purpose of government.[18]

And:

> The commodity sections were business operating Government business for the common good. . . . The war committees of industry knew, understood, and believed in the commodity chiefs. They were of the same piece.[19]

All in all, Clarkson exulted that thc commodity sections were "industry mobilized and drilled, responsive, keen, and fully staffed. They were militant and in serried ranks."[20]

The Chamber of Commerce was particularly enthusiastic over the war service committee system, a system that was to spur the trade association movement in peacetime as well. Chamber President Harry A. Wheeler, vice-president of the Union Trust Co. of Chicago, declared that:

> Creation of the War Service Committees promises to furnish the basis for a truly national organization of industry whose preparations and opportunities are unlimited. . . . The integration of business, the expressed aim of the National Chamber, is in sight. War is the stern teacher that is driving home the lesson of cooperative effort.[21]

---

[18] Ibid., p. 303.

[19] Ibid., pp. 300–01.

[20] Ibid., p. 309. On the War Industries Board, the commodity sections, and on big-business sentiment paving the path for the coordinated industry-government system, see James Weinstein, *The Corporate Ideal in the Liberal State, 1900–1918* (Boston: Beacon Press, 1969), p. 223 and passim.

[21] In *The Nation's Business* (August, 1918): 9–10. Quoted in Koistinen, "The 'Industrial-Military Complex' in Historical Perspective: World War I," pp. 392–93.

The result of all this new-found harmony within each industry, and between industry and government, was to "substitute cooperation for competition." Competition for government orders was virtually nonexistent, and "competition in price was practically done away with by Government action. Industry was for the time in . . . a golden age of harmony," and freed from the menace of business losses.[22]

One of the crucial functions of wartime planning was price-fixing, set in the field of industrial commodities by the Price-Fixing Committee of the War Industries Board. Beginning with such critical areas as steel and copper early in the war and then inexorably expanding to many other fields, the price-fixing was sold to the public as the fixing of maximum prices in order to protect the public against wartime inflation. In fact, however, the government set the price in each industry at such a rate as to guarantee a "fair profit" to the high-cost producers, thereby conferring a large degree of privilege and high profits upon the lower-cost firms.[23] Clarkson admitted that this system

> was a tremendous invigoration of big business and hard on small business. The large and efficient producers made larger profits than normally and many of the smaller concerns fell below their customary returns.[24]

But the higher-cost firms were largely content with their "fair profit" guarantee.

---

[22] Clarkson, *Industrial America in the World War*, p. 313.

[23] See George P. Adams, Jr., *Wartime Price Control* (Washington, D.C.: American Council on Public Affairs, 1942), pp. 57, 63–64. As an example, the government fixed the price of copper f.o.b. New York at 23 ½ cents per pound. The Utah Copper Co., which produced over 8 percent of the total copper output, had estimated costs of 11.8 cents per pound. In this way, Utah Copper was guaranteed nearly 100 percent profit on costs. Ibid., p. 64n.

[24] Clarkson, *Industrial America in the World War.*

The attitude of the Price-Fixing Committee was reflected in the statement of its Chairman, Robert S. Brookings, a retired lumber magnate, addressed to the nickel industry: "We are not in an attitude of envying you your profits; we are more in the attitude of justifying them if we can. That is the way we approach these things."[25]

Typical of the price-fixing operation was the situation in the cotton textile industry. Chairman Brookings reported in April, 1918, that the cotton goods committee had decided to "get together in a friendly way" to try to "stabilize the market." Brookings appended the feeling of the larger cotton manufacturers that it was better to fix a high long-run minimum price than to take full short-run advantage of the very high prices then in existence.[26]

The general enthusiasm of the business world, and especially big business, for the system of war collectivism can now he explained. The enthusiasm was a product of the resulting stabilization of prices, the ironing out of market fluctuations, and the fact that prices were almost always set by mutual consent of government and the representatives of each industry. It is no wonder that Harry A. Wheeler, president of the United States Chamber of Commerce, wrote in the summer of 1917 that war "is giving business the foundation for the kind of cooperative effort that alone can make the U.S. economically efficient." Or that the head of American Telephone and Telegraph hailed the perfecting of a "coordination to ensure complete cooperation not only between the Government and the companies, but between the companies themselves." The wartime cooperative planning was working so well, in fact, opined the chairman of

[25] Adams, *Wartime Price Control*, pp. 57–58.

[26] Weinstein, *The Corporate Ideal in the Liberal State, 1900–1918*, pp. 224–25.

the board of Republic Iron and Steel in early 1918, that it should be continued in peacetime as well.[27]

The vitally important steel industry is an excellent example of the workings of war collectivism. The hallmark of the closely knit control of the steel industry was the close "cooperation" between government and industry, a cooperation in which Washington decided on broad policy, and then left it up to Judge Elbert Gary, head of the leading steel producer, United States Steel, to implement the policy within the industry. Gary selected a committee representing the largest steel producers to help him run the industry. A willing ally was present in J. Leonard Replogle, head of American Vanadium Co. and chief of the Steel Division of the WIB. Replogle shared the long-standing desire of Gary and the steel industry for industrial cartelization and market stability under the aegis of a friendly federal government. Unsurprisingly, Gary was delighted with his new powers in directing the steel industry, and urged that he be given total power "to thoroughly mobilize and if necessary to commandeer." And *Iron Age*, the magazine of the iron and steel industry, exulted that

> it has apparently taken the most gigantic war in all history to give the idea of cooperation any such place in the general economic program as the country's steel manufacturers sought to give it in their own industry nearly ten years ago

with the short-lived *entente cordiale* between Judge Gary and President Roosevelt.[28]

---

[27] Melvin I. Urofsky, *Big Steel and the Wilson Administration* (Columbus: Ohio State University Press, 1969), pp. 152–53.

[28] Urofsky, *Big Steel and the Wilson Administration* , pp. 153–57. In his important study of business-government relations in the War Industries Board, Professor Robert Cuff has concluded that federal regulation of industry was shaped by big-business leaders, and that relations between government and

It is true that wartime relations between government and steel companies were sometimes strained, but the strain and the tough threat of government commandeering of resources was generally directed at smaller firms, such as Crucible Steel, which had stubbornly refused to accept government contracts.[29]

In the steel industry, in fact, it was the big steelmakers—U.S. Steel, Bethlehem, Republic, etc.—who, early in the war, had first urged government price-fixing, and they had to prod a sometimes confused government to adopt what eventually became the government's program. The main reason was that the big steel producers, happy at the enormous increase of steel prices in the market as a result of wartime demand, were anxious to stabilize the market at a high price and thus insure a long-run profit position for the duration of the war. The government—steel industry price-fixing agreement of September, 1917, was therefore hailed by John A. Topping, president of Republic Steel, as follows:

> The steel settlement will have a wholesome effect on the steel business because the principle of cooperative-regulation has been established with Government approval. Of course, present abnormal profits will be substantially reduced but a runaway market condition has been prevented and prosperity extended. . . . Furthermore, stability in future values should be conserved.[30]

Furthermore, the large steel firms were happy to use the fixed prices as a rationale for imposing controls and stability

---

big business were smoothest in those industries, such as steel, whose industrial leaders had already committed themselves to seeking government-sponsored cartelization. Robert D. Cuff, "Business, Government, and the War Industries Board" (Doctoral dissertation in history, Princeton University, 1966).

[29] Urofsky, *Big Steel and the Wilson Administration*, p. 154.

[30] In *Iron Age* (September 27, 1917). Quoted in Urofsky, *Big Steel and the Wilson Administration*, pp. 216–17

upon wages, which were also beginning to rise. The smaller steel manufacturers, on the other hand, often with higher costs, and who had not been as prosperous before the war, opposed price-fixing because they wished to take full advantage of the short-run profit bonanza brought about by the war.[31]

Under this regime, the steel industry achieved the highest level of profits in its history, averaging twenty-five percent per year for the two years of war. Some of the smaller steel companies, benefiting from their lower total capitalization, did almost twice as well.[32]

The most thoroughgoing system of price controls during the war was enforced not by the WIB but by the separate Food Administration, over which Herbert Clark Hoover presided as "Food Czar." The official historian of wartime price control justly wrote that the food control program "was the most important measure for controlling prices which the United States . . . had ever taken."[33]

Herbert Hoover accepted his post shortly after American entry into the war, but only on the condition that he alone have full authority over food, unhampered by boards or commissions. The Food Administration was established without legal authorization, and then a bill backed by Hoover was put through Congress to give the system the full force of law. Hoover was also given the power to requisition "necessaries,"

---

[31] Urofsky, *Big Steel and the Wilson Administration* , pp. 203–06. Also see Robert D. Cuff and Melvin I. Urofsky, "The Steel Industry and Price-Fixing During World War I," *Business History Review* (Autumn, 1970): 291–06.

[32] Urofsky, *Big Steel and the Wilson Administration*, pp. 228–33.

[33] Paul Willard Garrett, *Government Control Over Prices* (Washington, D.C.: Government Printing Office, 1920), p. 42.

to seize plants for government operation, and to regulate or prohibit exchanges.

The key to the Food Administration's system of control was a vast network of *licensing.* Instead of direct control over food, the FA was given the absolute power to issue licenses for any and all divisions of the food industry, and to set the conditions for keeping the license. Every dealer, every manufacturer, distributor, and warehouser of food commodities was required by Hoover to maintain its federal license.

A notable feature introduced by Hoover in his reign as Food Czar was the mobilization of a vast network of citizen volunteers as a mass of eager participants in enforcing his decrees. Thus, Herbert Hoover was perhaps the first American politician to realize the potential—in gaining mass acceptance and in enforcing government decrees—in the mobilizing of masses through a torrent of propaganda to serve as volunteer aides to the government bureaucracy. Mobilization proceeded to the point of inducing the public to brand as a virtual moral leper anyone dissenting from Mr. Hoover's edicts. Thus:

> The basis of all . . . control exercised by the Food Administration was the educational work which preceded and accompanied its measures of conservation and regulation. Mr. Hoover was committed thoroughly to the idea that the most effective method to control foods was to set every man, woman, and child in the country at the business of saving food. . . . The country was literally strewn with millions of pamphlets and leaflets designed to educate the people to the food situation. No war board at Washington was advertised as widely as the U.S. Food Administration. There were Food Administration insignia for the coat lapel, store window, the restaurant, the train, and the home. A real stigma was placed upon the person who was not loyal to Food Administration edicts through pressure by the schools,

> churches, women's clubs, public libraries, merchants' associations, fraternal organizations, and other social groups.[34]

The method by which the Food Administration imposed price control was its requirement that its licensees should receive "a reasonable margin of profit." This "reasonable margin" was interpreted as a margin over and above each producer's costs, and this cost-plus "reasonable profit" for each dealer became the rule of price control. The program was touted to the public as a means of keeping profits and food prices *down.* Although the Administration certainly wished to stabilize prices, the goal was also and more importantly to *cartelize.* Industry and government worked together to make sure that individual maverick competitors did not get out of line; prices in general were to be set at a level to guarantee a "reasonable" profit to everyone. The goal was not *lower* prices, but uniform, stabilized, non-competitive prices for all. The goal was far more to keep prices *up* than to keep them down. Indeed, any overly greedy competitor who tried to increase his profits above prewar levels by *cutting* his prices was dealt with most severely by the Food Administration.

Let us consider two of the most important food-control programs during World War I: wheat and sugar. Wheat price control, the most important program, came in the wake of wartime demand, which had pushed wheat prices up very rapidly to their highest level in the history of the United States. Thus, wheat increased by one dollar a bushel in the course of two months at the start of the war, reaching the unheard of price of three dollars a bushel. Control came in the wake of agitation that government must step in to thwart "speculators" by fixing maximum prices on wheat. Yet, under pressure by

---

[34] Garrett, *Government Control Over Prices*, p. 56.

the agriculturists, the government program fixed *by statute*, not maximum prices for wheat but *minima*; the Food Control Act of 1917 fixed a minimum price of two dollars a bushel for the next year's wheat crop. Not content with this special subsidy, the President proceeded to raise the minimum to two dollars and twenty-six cents a bushel in mid-1918, a figure that was then the precise market price for wheat. This increased minimum effectively fixed the price of wheat for the duration of the war. Thus, the government made sure that the consumers could not possibly benefit from any fall in wheat prices.

To enforce the artificially high price of wheat, Herbert Hoover established the Grain Corporation, "headed by practical grain men," which purchased the bulk of the wheat crop in the United States at the "fair price," and then resold the crop to the nation's flour mills at the same price. To keep the millers happy, the Grain Corporation guaranteed them against any possible losses from unsold stocks of wheat or flour. Moreover, each mill was guaranteed that its relative position in the flour industry would be maintained throughout the war. In this way, the flour industry was successfully cartelized through the instrument of government. Those few mills who balked at the cartel arrangement were dealt with handily by the Food Administration; as Garrett put it: "their operations . . . were reasonably well controlled . . . by the license requirements."[35]

The excessively high prices of wheat and flour also meant artificially high costs to the bakers. *They*, in turn, were taken under the cozy cartel umbrella by being required, in the name of "conservation," to mix inferior products with wheat flour at a fixed ratio. Each baker was of course delighted to comply with a requirement that he make inferior products, which he knew was also being enforced upon his competitors. Competition was also curtailed by the Food Administration's compulsory standardization of the sizes of bread loaves and by prohibiting price-cutting through discounts or

[35] Ibid., p. 66.

rebates to particular customers—the classic path toward the internal breakup of any cartel.[36]

In the particular case of sugar, there was a much more sincere effort to keep down prices—due to the fact that the United States was largely an importer rather than a producer of sugar. Herbert Hoover and the Allied governments duly formed an International Sugar Committee, which undertook to buy all of their countries' sugar, largely from Cuba, at an artificially low price, and then to allocate the raw sugar to the various refiners. Thus, the Allied governments functioned as a giant buying cartel to lower the price of their refiners' raw material.

Herbert Hoover instigated the plan for the International Sugar Committee, and the United States government appointed the majority of the five-man committee. As Chairman of the committee, Hoover selected Earl Babst, president of the powerful American Sugar Refining Co., and the other American members also represented refiner interests. The ISC promptly fixed a sharp reduction of the price of sugar: lowering the New York price of Cuban raw sugar from its high market price of six and three-quarter cents per pound in the summer of 1917 to six cents per pound. When the Cubans understandably balked at this artificially forced price reduction of their cash crop, the United States State Department and the Food Administration collaborated to coerce the Cuban government into agreement. Somehow, the Cubans were unable to obtain import licenses for needed wheat and coal from the United States Food Administration, and the result was a severe shortage of bread, flour, and coal in Cuba. Finally, the Cubans capitulated in mid-January, 1918, and the import licenses from the United States were

[36] Ibid., p. 73.

rapidly forthcoming.[37] Cuba also induced to prohibit all sugar exports except to the International Sugar Committee.

Apparently, Mr. Babst insured an extra bonus to his American Sugar Refining Company; for, shortly, officials of competing American refineries were to testify before Congress that this company had particularly profited from the activities of the International Sugar Committee and from the price that it fixed on Cuban sugar.[38]

Although the American government pursued with great diligence the goal of pushing down raw material prices for United States refiners, it also realized that it could not force down the price of raw sugar *too* low, since the government had to consider the marginal United States cane and beet-sugar producers, who had to receive their duly appointed "fair return." Jointly to harmonize and subsidize both the sugar refiners *and* the sugar growers in the United States, Mr. Hoover established a Sugar Equalization Board that would simultaneously keep the price of sugar *low* to Cuba while keeping it high enough for the American producers. The Board accomplished this feat by buying the Cuban sugar at the fixed low price and then reselling the crop to the refiners at a higher price to cover the American producers.[39]

The result of the artificially low prices for sugar was, inevitably, to create a severe sugar shortage by reducing supplies and by stimulating an excessive public consumption. The result was that sugar consumption was then severely restricted by federal rationing of sugar.

It is not surprising that the food industries were delighted with the wartime control program. Expressing the spirit of the

---

[37] See Robert F. Smith, *The United States and Cuba* (New York: Bookman Associates, 1960), pp. 20–21.

[38] Ibid., p. 191.

[39] Garrett, *Government Control Over Prices*, pp. 78–85.

entire war-collectivist regime, Herbert Hoover, in the words of Paul Garrett:

> maintained, as a cardinal policy from the beginning, a very close and intimate contact with the trade. The men, whom he chose to head his various commodity sections and responsible positions, were in a large measure tradesmen. . . . The determination of the policies of control within each branch of the food industry was made in conference with the tradesmen of that branch. . . . It might be said . . . that the framework of food control, as of raw material control, was built upon agreements with the trade. The enforcement of the agreements once made, moreover, was entrusted in part to the cooperation of constituted trade organizations. The industry itself was made to feel responsible for the enforcement of all rules and regulations.[40]

Also separate from the War Industries Board were the nation's railroads, which received the greatest single ministration of government dictation as compared to any other industry. The railroads, in fact, were seized and operated directly by the federal government.

As soon as the United States entered the war, the Administration urged the railroads to unite as one in behalf of the war effort. The railroads were delighted to comply and quickly formed what became known as the Railroads' War Board, promising faithfully to pursue a goal that they had long sought in peacetime: to cease competitive activities and to coordinate railroad operations.[41] Daniel Willard, president of the Baltimore & Ohio Railroad and Bernard Baruch's predecessor as head of the WIB, happily reported that the railroads had agreed to vest their War Board with complete authority to override individual

---

[40] Ibid. pp. 55–56.

[41] See K. Austin Kerr, *American Railroad Politics, 1914–1920* (Pittsburgh: University of Pittsburgh Press, 1968), pp. 44 ff.

railroad interests. Under its Chairman, Fairfax Harrison of the Southern Railroad, the War Board established a Committee on Car Service to coordinate national car supplies. Aiding the coordination effort was the Interstate Commerce Commission, the longtime federal regulatory body for the railroads. Once again, the government-promoted monopoly was an inspiration to many who were looking ahead to the peacetime economy. For several years the railroads had been agitating for "scientific management" as a means of achieving higher rates from the ICC and a governmentally imposed cartelization; but they had been thwarted by the pressure of the organized shippers, the industrial users of the railroads.

But now even the shippers were impressed. Max Thelen, chairman of the California Railroad Commission, president of the National Association of Railway and Utilities Commissions, and the leading spokesman for the organized shippers, agreed that the critical railroad problem was "duplication," and the "irrational" lack of complete inter-railroad coordination. And Senator Francis G. Newlands (D., Nev.), the most powerful congressman on railroad affairs as the chairman of a joint committee on transportation regulation, opined that the wartime experience was "somewhat shattering on old views regarding antitrust laws."[42]

Soon, however, it became clear that the system of voluntary private coordination was not really working well. Traffic departments of individual roads persisted in competitive practices; the railroad brotherhood unions were persistently demanding substantial wage increases; and the railroads and organized shippers locked horns over railroad demands for an across-the-board rate increase. All groups felt that regional coordination and overall efficiency would best be achieved by outright federal operation of the railroads. The shippers first proposed the scheme as a method of achieving coordination and to forestall

---

[42] Kerr, *American Railroad Politics, 1914–1920*, p. 48.

higher freight rates; the unions seconded the plan in order to obtain wage increases from the government; and the railroads cheerfully agreed when President Wilson assured them that each road would be guaranteed its 1916/17 profits—two years of unusually high profits for the railroad industry. With the federal government offering to take on the headaches of wartime dislocation and management, while granting the roads a very high guaranteed profit for doing nothing, why shouldn't the railroads leap to agreement?

The most enthusiastic Administration proponent of federal operation of the railroads was Secretary of the Treasury McAdoo, a former New York railroad executive and close associate of the Morgan interests, who in turn were the leading underwriters and owners of railroad bonds. McAdoo was rewarded by being named head of the United States Railroad Administration after Wilson seized the railroads on December 28, 1917.

Federal rule by the Morgan-oriented McAdoo proved to be a bonanza for the nation's railroads. Not only were the railroads now fully monopolized by direct government operation, but also the particular railroad executives now found themselves armed with the coercive power of the federal government. For McAdoo chose as his immediate assistants a group of top railroad executives, and all rate-setting powers of the ICC were shifted to the railroad-dominated Railroad Administration for the duration.[43] The significance of the shift is that the railroads,

[43] McAdoo's "cabinet," which assisted him in running the railroads, included Walker D. Hines and Edward Chambers, respectively chairman of the board and vice-president of the Santa Fe R.R.; Henry Walters, chairman of the board of the Atlantic Coast R.R.; Hale Holden, of the Burlington R.R.; A.H. Smith, president of the New York Central R.R.; John Barton Payne, formerly chief counsel of the Chicago Great Western R.R.; and Comptroller of the Currency John Skelton Williams, formerly chairman of the board of the Seaboard R.R. Hines was to be McAdoo's principal assistant; Payne became head of traffic. The Division of Operation was headed by Carl R.

although largely responsible for the inception and growth of the ICC as a cartelizing agency for the railroad industry, had seen control of the ICC slip into the hands of the organized shippers in the decade before the war. This had meant that the railroads had found it very difficult to win freight rate increases from the ICC. But now the wartime federal control of the railroads was shunting the shippers aside.[44]

McAdoo's brazen appointment of railroad men to virtually all the leading positions in the Railroad Administration, to the virtual exclusion of shippers and academic economists, greatly angered the shippers, who had launched an intense barrage of criticism of the system by midsummer of 1918. 'This barrage came to a head when McAdoo increasingly turned the direction of the RA, including the appointment of regional directors, over to his principal assistant, railroad executive Walker D. Hines. Shippers and ICC commissioners complained that

> railroad lawyers from the entire country descended on Washington, told their troubles to other railroad lawyers serving on McAdoo's staff, and were "told to go into an adjoining room and dictate what orders they want."[45]

As in the case of the War Industries Board, the railroad executives used their coercive governmental powers to deal a crippling blow to diversity and competition, on behalf of monopoly, in the name of "efficiency" and standardization. Again, over the opposition of shippers, the RA ordered the compulsory standardization of locomotive and equipment design, eliminated "duplicate" (i.e., competitive) passenger service and coal transportation, shut down off-line traffic offices, and

---

Gray, president of the Western Maryland R.R. One Unionist, W.S. Carter, head of the Brotherhood of Firemen and Engineers, was brought in to head the Division of Labor.

[44] Kerr, *American Railroad Politics, 1914–1920,* pp. 14–22.

[45] Ibid., p. 80.

ordered the cessation of competitive solicitation of freight by the railroads.

All of these edicts reduced railroad services to the hapless shippers. There were still other coerced reductions of service. One ended the shippers' privileges of specifying freight routes—and thereby of specifying the *cheapest* routes for shipping their goods. Another upset the peacetime practice of making the railroads liable for losses and damages to shipments; instead, the entire burden of proof was placed upon the shippers. Another RA ruling—the "sailing day plan"—ordered freight cars to remain in their terminals until filled, thus sharply curtailing service to small-town shippers.

The granting of absolute power to the railroad-dominated RA was cemented by the Federal Control Act of March, 1918, which *ex post facto* legalized the illegal federal takeover. Working closely with railroad lobbyists, the RA, backed by the full support of President Wilson, was able to drive through Congress the transfer of rate-making powers to itself from the ICC. Furthermore, all power was taken away from the invariably shipper-dominated state railroad commissions.

The RA hastened to exercise its rate-setting powers, announcing freight rate increases of twenty-five percent across the board in the spring of 1918—an act that permanently cemented shipper hostility to the system of federal operation. To add insult to injury, the new higher rates were set without any public hearings or consultation with other agencies or interests involved.

II

Historians have generally treated the economic planning of World War I as an isolated episode dictated by the requirements of the day and having little further significance. But, on the contrary, the war collectivism served as an inspiration and as a model for a mighty army of forces destined to forge the history of twentieth-century America. For big business, the wartime economy was a model of what could be achieved in national coordination and cartelization, in stabilizing production, prices, and profits, in replacing old-fashioned competitive laissez-faire by a system that they could broadly control and that would harmonize the claims of various powerful economic groups. It was a system that had already abolished much competitive diversity in the name of standardization. The wartime economy especially galvanized such business leaders as Bernard Baruch and Herbert Hoover, who would promote the cooperative "association" of business trade groups as Secretary of Commerce during the 1920s, an associationism that paved the way for the cooperative statism of Franklin Roosevelt's AAA and NRA.

The wartime collectivism also held forth a model to the nation's liberal intellectuals; for here was seemingly a system that replaced laissez-faire not by the rigors and class hatreds of proletarian Marxism, but by a new strong State, planning and organizing the economy in harmony with all leading economic groups. It was, not coincidentally, to be a neomercantilism, a "mixed economy," heavily staffed by these selfsame liberal intellectuals. And finally, both big business and the liberals saw in the wartime model a way to organize and integrate the often unruly labor force as a junior partner in the corporatist system—a force to be disciplined by their own "responsible" leadership of the labor unions.

For the rest of his life, Bernard Mannes Baruch sought to restore the lineaments of the wartime model. Thus, in summing up the experience of the WIB, Baruch extolled the fact that:

> many businessmen have experienced during the war, for the first time in their careers, the tremendous advantages, both to themselves and to the general public, of combination, of cooperation and common action…

Baruch called for the continuance of such corporate associations, in "inaugurating rules" to eliminate "waste" (i.e., competition), to exchange trade information, to agree on the channeling of supply and demand among themselves, to avoid "extravagant" forms of competition and to allocate the location of production. Completing the outlines of a corporate state, Baruch urged that such associations be governed by a federal agency, either the Department of Commerce or the Federal Trade Commission

> an agency whose duty it should be to encourage, under strict Government supervision, such cooperation and coordination . . .[46]

Baruch also envisioned a federal board for the retraining and channeling of labor after the war. At the very least, he urged standby legislation for price control and for industrial coordination and mobilization in the event of another war.[47]

During the 1920s and 1930s, Bernard Baruch served as a major inspiration of the drive toward a corporate state; moreover, many of the leaders of this drive were men who had served under him during the heady days of the WIB and who continued to function frankly as "Baruch's men" in national affairs. Thus, aided by Baruch, George N. Peek, of the Moline Plow Company, launched in the early 1920s the drive for farm price supports through federally organized farm cartels that was to culminate in President Hoover's Federal Farm Board in 1929 and then in Roosevelt's AAA. Peek's farm equipment business, of course, stood to benefit greatly from farm subsidies. Hoover appointed as first Chairman of the FFB none other than Baruch's old top aide from World War I, Alexander Legge of International Harvester, the leading farm machinery manufacturer. When Franklin Roosevelt created the AAA, he

[46] Bernard M. Baruch, *American Industry in the War* (New York: Prentice-Hall, 1941), pp. 105–06.

[47] Coit, *Mr. Baruch*, pp. 202–03, 218.

first offered the job of director to Baruch, and then gave the post to Baruch's man, George Peek.

Neither was Baruch laggard in promoting a corporatist system for industry as a whole. In the spring of 1930, Baruch proposed a peacetime reincarnation of the WIB as a "Supreme Court of Industry." In September of the following year, Gerard Swope, head of General Electric and brother of Baruch's closest confidant Herbert Bayard Swope, presented an elaborate plan for a corporate state that essentially revived the system of wartime planning. At the same time, one of Baruch's oldest friends, former Secretary William Gibbs McAdoo, was proposing a similar plan for a "Peace Industries Board." After Hoover dismayed his old associates by rejecting the plan, Franklin Roosevelt embodied it in the NRA, selecting Gerard Swope to help write the final draft, and picking another Baruch disciple and World War aide General Hugh S. Johnson—also of the Moline Plow Company—to direct this major instrument of state corporatism. When Johnson was fired, Baruch himself was offered the post.[48]

Other leading NRA officials were veterans of war mobilization. Johnson's chief of staff was another old friend of Baruch's, John Hancock, who had been Paymaster General of the Navy during the war and had headed the naval industrial program for the War Industries Board; other high officials of the NRA were Dr. Leo Wolman, who had been head of the production-statistics division of the WIB; Charles F. Homer, leader of the wartime Liberty Loan drive; and General Clarence C. Williams, who had been Chief of Ordnance in charge of Army war purchasing. Other WIB veterans highly placed in the New Deal were Isador Lubin, United States Commissioner of Labor Statistics in the New Deal; Captain Leon Henderson of the Ordinance Division of the WIB; and Senator Joseph Guffey (D., Pa.), who had worked in the WIB on conservation

[48] Ibid., pp. 440–43.

of oil, and who helped pattern the oil and coal controls of the New Deal on the wartime Fuel Administration.[49]

Another leading promoter of the new cooperation subsequent to his experience as wartime planner was Herbert Clark Hoover. As soon as the war was over, Hoover set out to "reconstruct America" along the lines of peacetime cooperation. He urged national planning through "voluntary" cooperation among businessmen and other economic groups under the "central direction" of the government. The Federal Reserve System was to allocate capital to essential industries and thereby to eliminate the competitive "wastes" of the free market. And in his term as Secretary of Commerce during the 1920s, Hoover assiduously encouraged the cartelization of industry through trade associations. In addition to inaugurating the modern program of farm price supports in the Federal Farm Board, Hoover urged the coffee buyers to form a cartel to lower buying prices; established a buying cartel in the rubber industry; led the oil industry in working toward restrictions on oil production in the name of "conservation"; tried repeatedly to raise prices, restrict production, and encourage marketing co-ops in the coal industry; and tried to force the cotton textile industry into a nationwide cartel to restrict production. Specifically in furtherance of the wartime abolition of thousands of diverse and competitive products, Hoover continued to impose standardization and "simplification" of materials and products during the 1920s. In this way, Hoover managed to abolish or "simplify" about a thousand industrial products. The "simplification" was worked out by the Department of Commerce in

---

[49] See William E. Leuchtenburg, "The New Deal and the Analogue of War," in John Braeman et al., eds., *Change and Continuity in Twentieth-Century America* (New York: Harper & Row, 1967), pp. 122–23.

collaboration with committees from each industry.[50] Grosvenor Clarkson hailed the fact that:

> it is probable that there will never again be such a multiplicity of styles and models in machinery and other heavy and costly articles as there was before the restrictions necessitated by the war... The ideas conceived and applied by the War Industries Board in war are being applied in peace by the Department of Commerce . . .[51]

Not the least of the influential groups dazzled and marked by the experience of war collectivism were the liberal intellectuals. Never before had so many intellectuals and academicians swarmed into government to help plan, regulate, and mobilize the economic system. The intellectuals served as advisers, technicians, framers of legislation, and administrators of bureaus. Furthermore, apart from the rewards of newly acquired prestige and power, the war economy held out to such intellectuals the promise of transforming the society into a "third way" completely different from the laissez-faire past that they scorned or the looming proletarian Marxism that they reviled and feared. Here was a planned corporate economy that seemed to harmonize all groups and classes under a strong and guiding nation-state with the liberals themselves at or near the helm. In a notable article, Professor Leuchtenburg saw the war collectivism

---

[50] See Herbert Hoover, *Memoirs* (New York: Macmillan, 1952), vol. 2, pp. 27, 66–70; on Hoover and the export industries, Joseph Brandes, *Herbert Hoover and Economic Diplomacy* (Pittsburgh: University of Pittsburgh Press, 1962); on the oil industry, Gerald D. Nash, *United States Oil Policy, 1890-1964* (Pittsburgh: University of Pittsburgh Press, 1968); on coal, Ellis W. Hawley, "Secretary Hoover and the Bituminous Coal Problem, 1921–1928," *Business History Review*(Autumn, 1968): 247–70; on cotton textiles, Louis Galambos, *Competition and Cooperation* (Baltimore: Johns Hopkins Press, 1966).

[51] Clarkson, *Industrial America in the World War*, pp. 484–85.

as "a logical outgrowth of the Progressive movement."[52] He demonstrated the enthusiasm of the Progressive intellectuals for the social transformation effected by the war. Thus, the *New Republic* hailed the "revolutionizing" of society by means of the war; John Dewey hailed the replacement of production for profit and "the absoluteness of private property" by production for use. Economists were particularly enchanted by the "notable demonstration of the power of war to force concert of effort and collective planning," and looked for "the same sort of centralized directing now employed to kill their enemies abroad for the new purpose of reconstructing their own life at home."[53]

Rexford Guy Tugwell, ever alert to the advance of social engineering, was soon to look back wistfully upon "America's wartime socialism"; lamenting the end of the war, he declared that "only the Armistice prevented a great experiment in control of production, control of price, and control of consumption." For, during the war, the old system of industrial competition had "melted away in the fierce new heat of nationalistic vision."[54]

Not merely the NRA and AAA, but virtually the entire New Deal apparatus—including the bringing to Washington of a host of liberal intellectuals and planners—owed its inspiration to the war collectivism of World War I. The Reconstruction Finance Corporation, founded by Hoover in 1932 and expanded by Roosevelt's New Deal, was a revival and expansion of the old War Finance Corporation, which had loaned government funds to munitions firms. Furthermore, Hoover, after

---

[52] Leuchtenburg, "The New Deal and the Analogue of War," p. 84n.

[53] Ibid., p. 89.

[54] Ibid., pp. 90–92. It was very similar considerations that also brought many liberal intellectuals, especially including those of the *New Republic*, into at least a temporary admiration for Italian Fascism. Thus, see John P. Diggins, "Flirtation with Fascism: American Pragmatic Liberals and Mussolini's Italy," *American Historical Review* (January, 1966): 487–506.

offering the post to Bernard Baruch, named as first Chairman of the RFC, Eugene Meyer, Jr., an old protégé of Baruch's, who had been managing director of the WFC. Much of the old WFC staff and method of operations were taken over bodily by the new agency. The Tennessee Valley Authority grew out of a wartime government nitrate and electric-power project at Muscle Shoals, and in fact included the old nitrate plant as one of its first assets. Moreover, many of the public power advocates in the New Deal had been trained in such wartime agencies as the Power Section of the Emergency Fleet Corporation. And even the innovative government corporate form of the TVA was based on wartime precedent.[55]

Wartime experience also provided the inspiration for the public housing movement of the New Deal. During the war, the Emergency Fleet Corp. and the United States Housing Corp. were established to provide housing for war workers. The war established the precedent of federal housing, and also trained architects like Robert Kohn, who functioned as chief of production for the housing division of the United States Shipping Board. After the war, Kohn exulted that "the war has put housing 'on the map' in this country"; and in 1933, Kohn was duly named by President Roosevelt to be the director of the New Deal's first venture into public housing. Furthermore, the Emergency Fleet Corp. and the United States Housing Corp. established large-scale public housing communities on planned "garden city" principles (Yorkship Village, N.J.; Union Park Gardens, Del.; Black Rock and Crane Tracts, Conn.), principles finally remembered and put into effect in the New Deal and afterward.[56]

The oil and coal controls established in the New Deal also rested on the precedent of the wartime Fuel Administration. Indeed, Senator Joseph Guffey (D., Pa.), leader in the coal

---

[55] Leuchtenburg, "The New Deal and the Analogue of War," pp. 109–10.
[56] Ibid., pp. 111–12.

and oil controls, had been head of the petroleum section of the War Industries Board.

Deeply impressed with the "national unity" and mobilization achieved during the war, the New Deal established the Civilian Conservation Corps to instill the martial spirit in America's youth. The idea was to take the "wandering boys" off the road and "mobilize" them into a new form of American Expeditionary Force. The Army, in fact, ran the CCC camps; CCC recruits were gathered at Army recruiting stations, equipped with World War I clothing, and assembled in army tents. The CCC, the New Dealers exulted, had given a new sense of meaning to the nation's youth, in this new "forestry army." Speaker Henry T. Rainey (D., Ill.) of the House of Representatives put it this way:

> They [the CCC recruits] are also under military training and as they come out of it . . . improved in health and developed mentally and physically and are more useful citizens . . . they would furnish a very valuable nucleus for an army.[57]

III

Particularly good evidence of the deep imprint of war collectivism was the reluctance of many of its leaders to abandon it when the war was finally over. Business leaders pressed for two postwar goals: continuance of government price-fixing to protect them against an expected postwar deflation; and a longer-range attempt to promote industrial cartelization in peacetime. In particular, businessmen wanted the price *maxima* (which had often served as *minima* instead) to be converted simply into outright minima for the postwar period. Wartime quotas to restrict pro-

---

[57] Ibid., p. 117. Roosevelt names union leader Robert Fechner, formerly engaged in war labor work, as director of the CCC to provide a civilian camouflage for the program, p. 115n.

duction, furthermore, needed only to remain in being to function as a frank cartelizing for raising prices in time of peace.

Accordingly, many of the industrial War Service Committees, and their WIB Section counterparts, urged the continuance of the WIB and its price-fixing system. In particular, section chiefs invariably urged continued price control in those industries that feared postwar deflation, while advocating a return to a free market wherever the specific industry expected a continuing boom. Thus, Professor Himmelberg concluded:

> Section chiefs in their recommendations to the Board consistently followed the wishes of their industries in urging protection if the industry expected price declines and release of all controls when the industry expected a favorable postwar market.[58]

Robert S. Brookings, Chairman of the Price-Fixing Committee of the WIB, declared that the WIB would be "as helpful . . . during the reconstruction period as we have during the war period in stabilizing values."[59]

From the big-business world, meanwhile, Harry A. Wheeler, president of the United States Chamber of Commerce, presented to Woodrow Wilson in early October, 1918, an ambitious scheme for a "Reconstruction Commission," to be composed of all the economic interests of the nation.

The WIB itself concurred, and urged the President to allow it to continue after the war. Baruch himself urged upon Wilson the continuation of at least the minimum price-fixing policies of the WIB. However, Baruch was gulling the public when he foresaw a postwar WIB as guarding against both inflation and deflation; there was no inclination to impose maximum prices against inflation.

---

[58] Robert F. Himmelberg, "The War Industries Board and the Antitrust Question in November 1918," *Journal of American History* (June, 1965): 65.

[59] Ibid.

The great problem with these ambitious plans of both industry and government was President Wilson himself. Perhaps a lingering attachment to the ideals, or at least to the rhetoric, of free competition prevented the President from giving any favorable attention to these postwar schemes.[60] The attachment was particularly nourished by Secretary of War Newton D. Baker, of all Wilson's advisers the closest to a believer in laissez-faire. Throughout October, 1918, Wilson rejected all of these proposals. The response of Baruch and the WIB was to put further pressure on Wilson during early November, by publicly predicting and urging that the WIB would definitely be needed during demobilization. Thus *The New York Times* reported, the day after the Armistice, that

> War Industries Board officials declared there would be much work for that organization to do. They foresee no serious industrial dislocation with the Government's grip on all war industries and material held tight.[61]

The President remained adamant, however, and on November 23 he ordered the complete disbanding of the WIB by the end of the year. The disappointed WIB officials accepted the decision without protest; partly because of expected congressional opposition to any attempt to continue, partly from the hostility to continued controls by those industries anticipating a boom. Thus, the shoe industry particularly chafed at any continuing controls.[62] The industries favoring controls, however, urged the WIB at least to ratify their own price *minima* and agreements for restricting production for the coming winter, and

---

[60] Ibid., pp. 63–64; Urofsky, *Big Steel and the Wilson Administration*, pp. 298–99.

[61] Quoted in Himmelberg, p. 64.

[62] Favoring continuing price controls were such industries as the chemical, iron and steel, lumber, and finished products generally. Opposing industries included abrasives, automotive products, and newspapers. Ibid., pp. 62, 65, 67.

to do so just before the disbandment of the agency. The Board was sorely tempted to engage in this final exploit, and indeed was informed by its legal staff that it could successfully continue such controls beyond the life of the agency even against the will of the President. The WIB, however, reluctantly turned down requests to this effect by the acid, zinc, and steel manufacturers on December 11.[63] It only rejected the price-fixing plans, however, because it feared being overturned by the courts should the Attorney General challenge such a decision.

One of the most ardent advocates of continued WIB price control was the great steel industry. Two days after the Armistice, Judge Gary of U.S. Steel urged the WIB to continue its regulations, and declared that "The members of the steel industry desire to cooperate with each other in every proper way . . ." Gary urged a three-month extension of price-fixing, with further gradual reductions that would prevent a return to "destructive" competition. Baruch replied that he was personally "willing to go to the very limit," but he was blocked by Wilson's attitude.[64]

If the WIB itself could not continue, perhaps the wartime cartelization could persist in other forms. During November, Arch W. Shaw, Chicago industrialist and head of the Conservation Division of the WIB (whose wartime work in fostering standardization was being transferred to the Department of Commerce) and Secretary of Commerce William Redfield agreed on a bill to allow manufacturers to collaborate in "the adoption of plans for the elimination of needless waste in the public interest," under the supervision of the Federal Trade Commission. When this proposal fizzled, Edwin B. Parker, Priorities Commissioner of the WIB, proposed in late November

---

[63] Urofsky, *Big Steel and the Wilson Administration*, pp. 306–07.

[64] Ibid., pp. 294–302.

a frankly cartelizing bill that would allow the majority of the firms in any given industry to set production quotas that would have to be obeyed by all the firms in that industry. The Parker plan won the approval of Baruch, Peek, and numerous other government officials and businessmen, but WIB's legal counsel warned that Congress would never give its consent.[65] Another proposal that interested Baruch was advanced by Mark Requa, Assistant Food Administrator, who proposed a United States Board of Trade to encourage and regulate industrial agreements that "promoted the national welfare."[66]

Whatever the reason, Bernard Baruch failed to press hard for these proposals, and so they died on the vine. If Baruch failed to press matters, however, his associate George Peek, head of the Finished Products Division of the WIB, was not so reticent. By mid-December, 1918, Peek wrote Baruch that the postwar era must retain the "benefits of proper cooperation." In particular,

> proper legislation should be enacted to permit cooperation in industry, in order that the lessons we have learned during the war may be capitalized . . . in peacetime. . . . Conservation; . . . standardization of products and processes, price fixing under certain conditions, etc., should continue with Government cooperation.[67]

By late December, Peek was proposing legislation for:

> some kind of an Emergency Peace Bureau . . . in order that businessmen may, in conjunction with such a Bu-

[65] Himmelberg, "The War Industries Board and the Antitrust Question in November 1918," pp. 70–71.

[66] Ibid., p. 72; Weinstein, *The Corporate Ideal in the Liberal State,* pp. 231–32.

[67] Himmelberg, "The War Industries Board and the Antitrust Question in November 1918," p. 72.

> reau, have an opportunity to meet and cooperate with Governmental cooperation . . .[68]

The leading business groups endorsed similar plans. In early December, the Chamber of Commerce of the United States called a meeting of the various industrial War Service Committees to convene as a "Reconstruction Congress of American Industry." The Reconstruction Congress called for revision of the Sherman Act to permit "reasonable" trade agreements under a supervisory body. Furthermore, a nationwide Chamber referendum, in early 1919, approved such a proposal by an overwhelming majority; and president Harry Wheeler urged the "cordial acceptance by organized business" of regulation that would ratify business agreements. The National Association of Manufacturers, before the war devoted to competition, warmly endorsed the same goals.

The last gasp of wartime cartelization came in February, 1919, with the establishment by the Department of Commerce of the Industrial Board.[69] Secretary of Commerce William C. Redfield, formerly president of the American Manufacturers Export Association, had long championed the view that government should promote and coordinate industrial cooperation. Redfield saw an entering wedge with the transfer of the WIB's Conservation Division to his department shortly after the Armistice. Redfield continued the wartime stimulation of trade associations, and to that end established an advisory board of former WIB officials. One of these advisers was George Peek; another

---

[68] Robert D. Cuff, "A 'Dollar-a-Year Man' in Government: George N. Peek and the War Industries Board," *Business History Review* (Winter, 1967): 417.

[69] On the Industrial Board, see Robert F. Himmelberg, "Business, Antitrust Policy, and the Industrial Board of the Department of Commerce, 1919," *Business History Review* (Spring, 1968): 1–23.

was Peek's assistant on the WIB, Ohio lumber executive William M. Ritter. It was Ritter, in fact, who originated the idea of the Industrial Board.

The Industrial Board, conceived by Ritter in January, 1919, and enthusiastically adopted and pushed by Secretary Redfield, was a cunning scheme. On its face, and as promoted to President Wilson and to others in the Administration and Congress, the Board was merely a device to secure large price *reductions*, and thereby to lower the inflated level of general prices and to stimulate consumer demand. It was therefore seemingly unrelated to the previous cartelizing drive and hence won the approval of the President, who established the new Board in mid-February. At Ritter's urging, George Peek was named chairman of the IB; other members included Ritter himself; George R. James, head of a major Memphis dry-goods concern and former chief of the Cotton and Cotton Linters section of the WIB; Lewis B. Reed, vice-president of the U.S. Silica Co. and another former assistant to Peek; steel castings manufacturer Samuel P. Bush, former head of the WIB's Facilities Division; Atlanta steel-fabricating manufacturer Thomas Glenn, also a veteran of the WIB; and two "outsiders," one representing the Labor Department and the other the Railroad Administration.

No sooner did the IB get under way than it pursued its real, but previously camouflaged, purpose: not to reduce, but rather to stabilize prices at existing high levels. Moreover, the method of stabilization would be the longed-for but previously rejected path of ratifying industrial price agreements arrived at in collaboration with the Board. Deciding on this cartelizing policy in early March, the IB moved toward the first application in a conference with, unsurprisingly, the steel industry on March 19-20, 1919. Opening the conference, Chairman George Peek grandly declared that the event might prove "epoch-making," especially in establishing "real genuine cooperation between Government, industry, and labor, so that we may eliminate the possibility of the destructive forces . . ."[70] The steel men were of course delighted, hailing the "great chance . . . to come into close contact with the Government itself . . ."[71] The IB told the steel industry that any agreement to sustain prices agreed upon by the conference would be immune from the antitrust laws. Not only was the price list offered by the IB to the steel men still very high even if moderately lower than existing prices; but Peek agreed to announce to the public that steel prices would not be lowered further for the remainder of the year. Peek advised the steel men that his statement would be their biggest asset; for "I don't know what I wouldn't have given in times past if in my own business I could say that the government of the United States says this is as low a price as you could get."[72]

The IB-steel agreement lowered steel prices by a modest ten to fourteen percent. The small, high-cost steel producers were disgruntled, but the big steel firms welcomed the agreement as a coordinated, orderly reduction of inflated prices, and especially welcomed the Board's guarantee of the fixed price for the remainder of the year.

The elated IB proceeded with similar conferences for the coal and building materials industries, but two dark clouds promptly appeared: the refusal of the government's own Railroad Administration to pay the fixed, agreed-upon price for steel rails and for coal; and the concern of the Justice Department for the evident violation of the antitrust laws. The railroad men running the RA particularly balked at the reduced but still high price that they were going to be forced to pay for steel rails—at a rate that they declared was at least two dollars per

---

[70] Himmelberg, "Industrial Board," p. 13.

[71] Professor Urofsky surmised from the orderly and very moderate price reductions in steel during the first months of 1919 that Robert S. Brookings had quietly given the steel industry the green light to proceed with its own price-fixing. Urofsky, *Big Steel and the Wilson Administration*, pp. 307–08.

[72] Himmelberg, "Industrial Board," p. 14n.

ton above the free-market price. Walker D. Hines, head of the RA, denounced the IB as a price-fixing agency, dominated by steel and other industries, and he called for the abolition of the Industrial Board. This call was seconded by the powerful Secretary of the Treasury Carter Glass. The Attorney General concurred that the IB's policy was illegal price-fixing and in violation of the antitrust laws. Finally, President Wilson dissolved the Industrial Board in early May, 1919; wartime industrial planning had at last been dissolved, its formal cartelization to reappear a decade and a half later.

Yet remnants of wartime collectivism still remained. The high wartime minimum wheat price of two dollars and twenty-six cents a bushel was carried over to the 1919 crop, continuing until June, 1920. But the most important carry-over of war collectivism was the Railroad Administration: the government's operation of the nation's railroads. When William Gibbs McAdoo resigned as head of the RA at the end of the war, he was succeeded by the previous *de facto* operating head, railroad executive Walker D. Hines. There was no call for immediate return to private operation, because the railroad industry generally agreed upon drastic regulation to curb or eliminate "wasteful" railroad competition and coordinate the industry, to fix prices to insure a "fair profit," and to outlaw strikes through compulsory arbitration. This was the overall thrust of railroad sentiment. Furthermore, being in effective control of the RA, the roads were in no hurry to return to private operation and jurisdiction by the less reliable ICC. Although McAdoo's plan to postpone by five years the given 1920 date for return to private operation gained little support, Congress proceeded to use its time during 1919 to tighten the monopolization of the railroads.

In the name of "scientific management," Senator Albert Cummins (R., Iowa) proceeded to grant the railroads' fondest dreams. Cummins' bill, warmly approved by Hines and railroad executive Daniel Willard, ordered the consolidation of numerous railroads and would set the railroad rates according to a "fair," fixed return on capital investment. Strikes would be outlawed, and all labor disputes settled by compulsory arbitration. For their part, the Association of Railroad Executives submitted a legislative plan similar to the Cummins Bill. Also similar to the Cummins Bill was the proposal of the National Association of Owners of Railroad Securities, a group composed largely of savings banks and insurance companies. In contrast to these plans, the Citizens National Railroad League, consisting of individual railroad investors, proposed coerced consolidation into one national railroad corporation, and the guaranteeing of minimum earnings to this new road.

All of these plans were designed to tip the prewar balance sharply in favor of the railroads and against the shippers, and, as a result, the Cummins Bill, in passing the Senate, ran into trouble in the House. The trouble was fomented by the shippers, who demanded a return to the status quo ante when the shipper-dominated ICC was in charge. Furthermore, for their part the wartime experience had embittered the shippers, who, along with the ICC itself, demanded a return to the higher quality service provided by railroad competition rather than the increased monopolization provided by the various railroad bills. Unsurprisingly, however, one of the leading nonrailroad business groups favoring the Cummins Bill was the Railway Business Association, a group of manufacturers and distributors of railroad supplies and equipment. The House of Representatives, in its turn, passed the Esch Bill, which essentially reestablished the prewar rule of the ICC.

President Wilson had put pressure on Congress to make a decision by threatening the return of the railroads to private operation by the given date of January 1, 1920, but, under pressure of the railroads who were anxious to push the Cummins Bill, Wilson extended the deadline to March 1. Finally, the joint conference committee of Congress reported out the Transportation Act of 1920, a compromise that was essentially the Esch Bill returning the railroads to the prewar ICC, but adding the Cummins provisions for a two-year guarantee to the railroads to set rates providing a "fair return" of five and a half percent on investment. Furthermore, on the agreement of both shippers and the roads, the power to set *minimum* railroad rates was now granted to the ICC. This agreement was the product of railroads eager to set a floor under freight rates, and shippers anxious to protect budding canal transportation against railroad competition. Furthermore, although railway union objections blocked the provision for the outlawing of strikes, a Railroad Labor Board was established to try to settle labor disputes.[73]

With the return of the railroads to private operation in March, 1920, war collectivism finally and at long last seemed to pass from the American scene. But pass it never really did; for the inspiration and the model that it furnished for a corporate state in America continued to guide Herbert Hoover and other leaders in the 1920s, and was to return full-blown in the New Deal, and in the World War II economy. In fact, it supplied the broad outlines for the Corporate Monopoly State that the New Deal was to establish, seemingly permanently, in the United States of America.

[73] On the maneuvering leading to the Transportation Act of 1920, see Kerr, *American Railroad Politics, 1914–1920*, pp. 128–227.

II

World War I as Fulfillment: Power and the Intellectuals

INTRODUCTION

In contrast to older historians who regarded World War I as the destruction of progressive reform, I am convinced that the war came to the United States as the "fulfillment," the culmination, the veritable apotheosis of progressivism in American life.[1] I regard progressivism as basically a movement on behalf of Big Government in all walks of the economy and society, in a fusion or coalition between various groups of big businessmen, led by the House of Morgan, and rising groups of technocratic and statist intellectuals. In this fusion, the values and interests of both groups would be pursued through government.

---

[1] An earlier version of this paper was delivered at a Pacific Institute Conference on "Crisis and Leviathan," at Menlo Park, Calif., October 1986. It appeared in print in *the Journal of Libertarian Studies* 9, no. 1 (Winter, 1989). It was reprinted in John V. Denson, ed., *The Costs of War: America's Pyrrhic Victories* (New Brunswick, N.J.: Transaction Publishers, 1997). The title of this paper is borrowed from the pioneering last chapter of James Weinstein's excellent work, *The Corporate Ideal in the Liberal State, 1900–1918* (Boston: Beacon Press, 1968). The last chapter is entitled, "War as Fulfillment."

Big business would be able to use the government to cartelize the economy, restrict competition, and regulate production and prices, and also to be able to wield a militaristic and imperialist foreign policy to force open markets abroad and apply the sword of the State to protect foreign investments. Intellectuals would be able to use the government to restrict entry into their professions and to assume jobs in Big Government to apologize for, and to help plan and staff, government operations. Both groups also believed that, in this fusion, the Big State could be used to harmonize and interpret the "national interest" and thereby provide a "middle way" between the extremes of "dog-eat-dog" laissez faire and the bitter conflicts of proletarian Marxism.

Also animating both groups of progressives was a post-millennial pietist Protestantism that had conquered "Yankee" areas of northern Protestantism by the 1830s and had impelled the pietists to use local, state, and finally federal governments to stamp out "sin," to make America and eventually the world holy, and thereby to bring about the Kingdom of God on earth. The victory of the Bryanite forces at the Democratic national convention of 1896 destroyed the Democratic Party as the vehicle of "liturgical" Roman Catholics and German Lutherans devoted to personal liberty and laissez faire and created the roughly homogenized and relatively non-ideological party system we have today. After the turn of the century, this development created an ideological and power vacuum for the expanding number of progressive technocrats and administrators to fill. In that way, the locus of government shifted from the legislature, at least partially subject to democratic check, to the oligarchic and technocratic executive branch.

World War I brought the fulfillment of all these progressive trends. Militarism, conscription, massive intervention at home and abroad, a collectivized war economy, all came about during the war and created a mighty cartelized system that most of its leaders spent the rest of their lives trying to recreate, in peace as well as war. In the World War I chapter of his outstanding work, *Crisis and Leviathan*, Professor Robert Higgs concentrates on the war economy and illuminates the interconnections with conscription.

In this paper, I would like to concentrate on an area that Professor Higgs relatively neglects: the coming to power during the war of the various groups of progressive intellectuals.[2] I use the term "intellectual" in the broad sense penetratingly described by F.A. Hayek: that is, not merely theorists and academicians, but also all manner of opinion-molders in society—writers, journalists, preachers, scientists, activists of all sort—what Hayek calls "secondhand dealers in ideas."[3] Most of these intellectuals, of whatever strand or occupation, were either dedicated, messianic postmillennial pietists or else former pietists, born in a deeply pietist home, who, though now secularized, still possessed an intense messianic belief in national and world salvation through Big Government. But, in addition, oddly but characteristically, most combined in their thought and agitation messianic moral or religious fervor with an empirical, allegedly *value-free*, and strictly *scientific* devotion to social science. Whether it be the medical profession's combined scientific and moralistic devotion to stamping out sin or a similar position among economists or philosophers, this blend is typical of progressive intellectuals.

In this paper, I will be dealing with various examples of individual or groups of progressive intellectuals, exulting in the

---

[2] Robert Higgs, *Crisis and Leviathan* (New York: Oxford University Press, 1987), pp. 123–58. For my own account of the collectivized war economy of World War I, see Murray N. Rothbard, "War Collectivism in World War I," in R. Radosh and M. Rothbard. eds., *A New History of Leviathan: Essays on the Rise of the American Corporate State* (New York: Dutton. 1972), pp. 66–110.

[3] F.A. Hayek, "The Intellectuals and Socialism," in *Studies in Philosophy, Politics and Economics* (Chicago: University of Chicago Press, 1967), pp. 178ff.

triumph of their creed and their own place in it, as a result of America's entry into World War I. Unfortunately, limitations of space and time preclude dealing with all facets of the wartime activity of progressive intellectuals; in particular, I regret having to omit treatment of the conscription movement, a fascinating example of the creed of the "therapy" of "discipline" led by upper-class intellectuals and businessmen in the J.P. Morgan ambit.[4] I shall also have to omit both the highly significant trooping to the war colors of the nation's preachers, and the wartime impetus toward the permanent centralization of scientific research.[5]

There is no better epigraph for the remainder of this paper than a congratulatory note sent to President Wilson after the delivery of his war message on April 2, 1917. The note was sent by Wilson's son-in-law and fellow Southern pietist and progressive, Secretary of the Treasury William Gibbs McAdoo, a man who had spent his entire life as an industrialist in New York City, solidly in the J.P. Morgan ambit. McAdoo wrote to Wilson: "You have done a great thing nobly! I firmly believe that it is God's will that America should do this transcendent service for humanity throughout the world and that

[4] On the conscription movement, see in particular Michael Pearlman, *To Make Democracy Safe for America: Patricians and Preparedness in the Progressive Era* (Urbana: University of Illinois Press, 1984). See also John W. Chambers II, "Conscripting for Colossus: The Adoption of the Draft in the United States in World War I," Ph.D. diss., Columbia University, 1973; John Patrick Finnegan, *Against the Specter of a Dragon: The Campaign for American Military Preparedness, 1914–1917* (Westport, Conn.: Greenwood Press, 1974); and John Gany Clifford, *The Citizen Soldiers: The Plattsburg Training Camp Movement* (Lexington: University Press of Kentucky, 1972).

[5] On ministers and the war, see Ray H. Abrams, *Preachers Present Arms* (New York: Round Table Press, 1933). On the mobilization of science, see David F. Noble, *America By Design: Science, Technology and the Rise of Corporate Capitalism* (New York: Oxford University Press, 1977), and Ronald C. Tobey, *The American Ideology of National Science, 1919–1930* (Pittsburgh: University of Pittsburgh Press, 1971).

you are His chosen instrument."[6] It was not a sentiment with which the president could disagree.

PIETISM AND PROHIBITION

One of the few important omissions in Professor Higgs's book is the crucial role of postmillennial pietist Protestantism in the drive toward statism in the United States. Dominant in the "Yankee" areas of the North from the 1830s on, the aggressive "evangelical" form of pietism conquered Southern Protestantism by the 1890s and played a crucial role in progressivism after the turn of the century and through World War I. Evangelical pietism held that requisite to any man's salvation is that he do his best to see to it that everyone else is saved, and doing one's best inevitably meant that the State must become a crucial instrument in maximizing people's chances for salvation. In particular, the State plays a pivotal role in stamping out sin, and in "making America holy." To the pietists, sin was very broadly defined as any force that might cloud men's minds so that they could not exercise their theological free will to achieve salvation. Of particular importance were slavery (until the Civil War), Demon Rum, and the Roman Catholic Church, headed by the Antichrist in Rome. For decades after the Civil War, "rebellion" took the place of slavery in the pietist charges against their great political enemy, the Democratic party.[7] Then in

---

[6] Cited in Gerald Edward Markowitz, "Progressive Imperialism: Consensus and Conflict in the Progressive Movement on Foreign Policy, 1898–1917." Ph.D. diss., University of Wisconsin, 1971, p. 375, an unfortunately neglected work on a highly important topic.

[7] Hence the famous imprecation hurled at the end of the 1884 campaign that brought the Democrats into the presidency for the first time since the Civil War, that the Democratic Party was the party of "Rum, Romanism, and Rebellion." In that one phrase, the New York Protestant minister was able to sum up the political concerns of the pietist movement.

1896, with the evangelical conversion of Southern Protestantism and the admission to the Union of the sparsely populated and pietist Mountain states, William Jennings Bryan was able to put together a coalition that transformed the Democrats into a pietist party and ended forever that party's once proud role as the champion of *liturgical* (Catholic and High German Lutheran) Christianity and of personal liberty and laissez faire.[8]

The pietists of the nineteenth and early twentieth centuries were all postmillennialist: They believed that the Second Advent of Christ will occur only *after* the millennium—a thousand years of the establishment of the Kingdom of God on earth—has been brought about by human effort. Postmillennialists have therefore tended to be statists, with the State becoming an important instrument of stamping out sin and Christianizing the social order so as to speed Jesus's return.[9]

---

[8] For an introduction to the growing literature of "ethnoreligious" political history in the United States, see Paul Kleppner, *The Cross of Culture* (New York: the Free Press, 1970); and idem, *The Third Electoral System, 1853–1892* (Chapel Hill: University of North Carolina Press, 1979). For the latest research on the formation of the Republican Party as a pietist party, reflecting the interconnected triad of pietist concerns—antislavery, prohibition, and anti-Catholicism—see William E. Gienapp, "Nativism and the Creation of a Republican Majority in the North before the Civil War," *Journal of American History* 72 (December 1985): 529–559.

[9] Orthodox Augustinian Christianity, as followed by the liturgicals, is "a-millennialist," i.e., it believes that the "millennium" is simply a metaphor for the emergence of the Christian Church and that Jesus will return without human aid and at his own unspecified time. Modern "fundamentalists," as they have been called since the early years of the twentieth century, are "premillennialists," i.e., they believe that Jesus will return to usher in a thousand years of the Kingdom of God on Earth, a time marked by various "tribulations" and by Armageddon, until history is finally ended. Premillennialists, or "millennarians," do not have the statist drive of the postmillennialists; instead, they tend to focus on predictions and signs of Armageddon and of Jesus's advent.

Professor Timberlake neatly sums up this politico-religious conflict:

> Unlike those extremist and apocalyptic sects that rejected and withdrew from the world as hopelessly corrupt, and unlike the more conservative churches, such as the Roman Catholic, Protestant Episcopal, and Lutheran, that tended to assume a more relaxed attitude toward the influence of religion in culture, evangelical Protestantism sought to overcome the corruption of the world in a dynamic manner, not only by converting men to belief in Christ but also by Christianizing the social order through the power and force of law. According to this view, the Christian's duty was to use the secular power of the state to transform culture so that the community of the faithful might be kept pure and the work of saving the unregenerate might be made easier. Thus the function of law was not simply to restrain evil but to educate and uplift.[10]

Both prohibition and progressive reform were pietistic, and as both movements expanded after 1900 they became increasingly intertwined. The Prohibition Party, once confined—at least in its platform—to a single issue, became increasingly and frankly progressive after 1904. The Anti-Saloon League, the major vehicle for prohibitionist agitation after 1900, was also markedly devoted to progressive reform. Thus at the League's annual convention in 1905, Rev. Howard H. Russell rejoiced in the growing movement for progressive reform and particularly hailed Theodore Roosevelt, as that "leader of heroic mould, of absolute honesty of character and purity of life, that foremost man of this world. . . ."[11] At the Anti-Saloon League's convention of 1909, Rev. Purley A. Baker lauded the labor union

---

[10] James H. Timberlake, *Prohibition and the Progressive Movement, 1900–1920* (New York: Atheneum, 1970), pp. 7–8.

[11] Quoted in Timberlake, *Prohibition*, p. 33.

movement as a holy crusade for justice and a square deal. The League's 1915 convention, which attracted 10,000 people, was noted for the same blend of statism, social service, and combative Christianity that had marked the national convention of the Progressive Party in 1912.[12] And at the League's June 1916 convention, Bishop Luther B. Wilson stated, without contradiction, that everyone present would undoubtedly hail the progressive reforms then being proposed.

During the Progressive years, the Social Gospel became part of the mainstream of pietist Protestantism. Most of the evangelical churches created commissions on social service to promulgate the Social Gospel, and virtually all of the denominations adopted the Social Creed drawn up in 1912 by the Commission of the Church and Social Service of the Federal Council of Churches. The creed called for the abolition of child labor, the regulation of female labor, the right of labor to organize (i.e., compulsory collective bargaining), the elimination of

---

[12] The Progressive Party convention was a mighty fusion of all the major trends in the progressive movement: statist economists, technocrats, social engineers, social workers, professional pietists, and partners of J.P. Morgan & Co. Social Gospel leaders Lyman Abbon, the Rev. R. Heber Newton and the Rev. Washington Gladden, were leading Progressive Party delegates. The Progressive Party proclaimed itself as the "recrudescence of the religious spirit in American political life." Theodore Roosevelt's acceptance speech was significantly entitled "A Confession of Faith," and his words were punctuated by "amens" and by a continual singing of pietist Christian hymns by the assembled delegates. They sang "Onward Christian Soldiers," "The Battle Hymn of the Republic," and especially the revivalist hymn, "Follow, Follow, We Will Follow Jesus," with the word "Roosevelt" replacing "Jesus" at every turn. The horrified *New York Times* summed up the unusual experience by calling the Progressive grouping "a convention of fanatics." And it added, "It was not a convention at all. It was an assemblage of religious enthusiasts. It was such a convention as Peter the Hermit held. It was a Methodist camp following done over into political terms." Cited in John Allen Gable, *The Bull Moose Years: Theodore Roosevelt and the Progressive Party* (Port Washington, N.Y.: Kennikat Press, 1978), p. 75.

poverty, and an "equitable" division of the national product. And right up there as a matter of social concern was the liquor problem. The creed maintained that liquor was a grave hindrance toward the establishment of the Kingdom of God on earth, and it advocated the "protection of the individual and society from the social, economic, and moral waste of the liquor traffic.[13]

The Social Gospel leaders were fervent advocates of statism and of prohibition. These included Rev. Walter Rauschenbusch and Rev. Charles Stelzle, whose tract *Why Prohibition!* (1918) was distributed, after the United States's entry into World War I, by the Commission on Temperance of the Federal Council of Churches to labor leaders, members of Congress, and important government officials. A particularly important Social Gospel leader was Rev. Josiah Strong, whose monthly journal, *The Gospel of the Kingdom*, was published by Strong's American Institute of Social Service. In an article supporting prohibition in the July 1914 issue, *The Gospel of the Kingdom* hailed the progressive spirit that was at last putting an end to "personal liberty":

> "Personal Liberty" is at last an uncrowned, dethroned king, with no one to do him reverence. The social consciousness is so far developed and is becoming so autocratic, that institutions and governments must give heed to its mandate and share their life accordingly. We are no longer frightened by that ancient bogy—"paternalism in government." We affirm boldly, it is the business of government to be just that—Paternal. *Nothing human can be foreign to a true government.*[14]

[13] Timberlake, *Prohibition*, p. 24.

[14] Quoted in Timberlake, *Prohibition*, p. 27. Italics in the article. Or, as the Rev. Stelzle put it, in *Why Prohibition*!, "There is no such thing as an absolute individual right to do any particular thing, or to eat or drink any particular thing, or to enjoy the association of one's own family, or even to live, if that

As true crusaders, the pietists were not content to stop with the stamping out of sin in the United States alone. If American pietism was convinced that Americans were God's chosen people, destined to establish a Kingdom of God within the United States, surely the pietists' religious and moral duty could not stop there. In a sense, the world was America's oyster. As Professor Timberlake put it, once the Kingdom of God was in the course of being established in the United States,

> it was therefore America's mission to spread these ideals and institutions abroad so that the Kingdom could be established throughout the world. American Protestants were accordingly not content merely to work for the kingdom of God in America, but felt compelled to assist in the reformation of the rest of the world also.[15]

American entry into World War I provided the fulfillment of prohibitionist dreams. In the first place, all food production was placed under the control of Herbert Hoover, Food Administration czar. But if the US government was to control and allocate food resources, shall it permit the precious scarce supply of grain to be siphoned off into the "waste," if not the sin, of the manufacture of liquor? Even though less than two percent of American cereal production went into the manufacture of alcohol, think of the starving children of the world who might otherwise be fed. As the progressive weekly the *Independent* demagogically phrased it. "Shall the many have food, or the few have drink?" For the ostensible purpose of "conserving" grain, Congress wrote an amendment into the Lever Food and Fuel Control Act of August 10, 1917, that absolutely prohibited the use of foodstuffs, hence grain, in the production of alcohol. Congress would have added a prohibition on the

---

thing is in conflict with the law of public necessity." Quoted in David E. Kyvig, *Repealing National Prohibition* (Chicago: University of Chicago Press, 1979), p. 9.

[15] Timberlake, *Prohibition*, pp. 37–38.

manufacture of wine or beer, but President Wilson persuaded the Anti-Saloon League that he could accomplish the same goal more slowly and thereby avoid a delaying filibuster by the wets in Congress. However, Herbert Hoover, a progressive and a prohibitionist, persuaded Wilson to issue an order, on December 8, both greatly reducing the alcoholic content of beer and limiting the amount of foodstuffs that could be used in its manufacture.[16]

The prohibitionists were able to use the Lever Act and war patriotism to good effect. Thus, Mrs. W. E. Lindsey, wife of the governor of New Mexico, delivered a speech in November 1917 that noted the Lever Act, and declared:

> Aside from the long list of awful tragedies following in the wake of the liquor traffic, the economic waste is too great to be tolerated at this time. With so many people of the allied nations near to the door of starvation, it would be criminal ingratitude for us to continue the manufacture of whiskey.[17]

Another rationale for prohibition during the war was the alleged necessity to protect American soldiers from the dangers of alcohol to their health, their morals, and their immortal souls. As a result, in the Selective Service Act of May 18, 1917, Congress provided that dry zones must be established around every army base, and it was made illegal to sell or even to give liquor to any member of the military establishment within those

[16] See David Burner, *Herbert Hoover: A Public Life* (New York: Alfred A. Knopf, 1979), p. 107.

[17] James A. Burran, "Prohibition in New Mexico, 1917." *New Mexico Historical Quarterly* 48 (April 1973): 140–141. Mrs. Lindsey of course showed no concern whatever for the German, allied, and neutral countries of Europe being subjected to starvation by the British naval blockade. The only areas of New Mexico that resisted the prohibition crusade in the referendum in the November 1917 elections were the heavily Hispanic-Catholic districts.

zones, even in one's private home. Any inebriated servicemen were subject to courts-martial.

But the most severe thrust toward national prohibition was the Anti-Saloon League's proposed eighteenth constitutional amendment, outlawing the manufacture, sale, transportation, import or export of all intoxicating liquors. It was passed by Congress and submitted to the states at the end of December 1917. Wet arguments that prohibition would prove unenforceable were met with the usual dry appeal to high principle: Should laws against murder and robbery he repealed simply because they cannot be completely enforced? And arguments that private property would be unjustly confiscated were also brushed aside with the contention that property injurious to the health, morals, and safety of the people had always been subject to confiscation without compensation.

When the Lever Act made a distinction between hard liquor (forbidden) and beer and wine (limited), the brewing industry tried to save their skins by cutting themselves loose from the taint of distilled spirits. "The true relationship with beer," insisted the United States Brewers Association, "is with light wines and soft drinks-not with hard liquors." The brewers affirmed their desire to "sever, once for all, the shackles that bound our wholesome productions to ardent spirits." But this craven attitude would do the brewers no good. After all, one of the major objectives of the drys was to smash the brewers, once and for all, they whose product was the very embodiment of the drinking habits of the hated German-American masses, both Catholic and Lutheran, liturgicals and beer drinkers all. German-Americans were now fair game. Were they not all agents of the satanic Kaiser, bent on conquering the world? Were they not conscious agents of the dreaded Hun *Kultur*, out to destroy American civilization? And were not most brewers German?

And so the Anti-Saloon League thundered that "German brewers in this country have rendered thousands of men inefficient and are thus crippling the Republic in its war on Prussian militarism." Apparently, the Anti-Saloon League took no heed of the work of German brewers in Germany, who were presumably performing the estimable service of rendering "Prussian militarism" helpless. The brewers were accused of being pro-German, and of subsidizing the press (apparently it was all right to be pro-English or to subsidize the press if one were not a brewer). The acme of the accusations came from one prohibitionist: "We have German enemies," he warned, "in this country too. And the worst of all our German enemies, the most treacherous, the most menacing are Pabst, Schlitz, Blatz, and Miller."[18]

In this sort of atmosphere, the brewers didn't have a chance, and the Eighteenth Amendment went to the states, outlawing all forms of liquor. Since twenty-seven states had already outlawed liquor, this meant that only nine more were needed to ratify this remarkable amendment, which directly involved the federal constitution in what had always been, at most, a matter of police power of the states. The thirty-sixth state ratified the Eighteenth Amendment on January 16, 1919, and by the end of February all but three states (New Jersey, Rhode Island, and Connecticut) had made liquor unconstitutional as well as illegal. Technically, the amendment went into force the following January, but Congress speeded matters up by passing the War Prohibition Act of November 11, 1918, which banned the manufacture of beer and wine after the following May and outlawed the sale of all intoxicating beverages after June 30, 1919, a ban to continue in effect until the end of demobilization. Thus total national prohibition really began on July 1, 1919, with the Eighteenth Amendment taking over six months later. The constitutional amendment needed a congressional enforcing act, which Congress supplied with the Volstead (or National Prohibition) Act, passed over Wilson's veto at the end of October 1919.

---

[18] Timberlake, *Prohibition*, p. 179.

With the battle against Demon Rum won at home, the restless advocates of pietist prohibitionism looked for new lands to conquer. Today America, tomorrow the world. In June 1919 the triumphant Anti-Saloon League called an international prohibition conference in Washington and created a World League Against Alcoholism. World prohibition, after all, was needed to finish the job of making the world safe for democracy. The prohibitionists' goals were fervently expressed by Rev. A.C. Bane at the Anti-Saloon League's 1917 convention, when victory in America was already in sight. To a wildly cheering throng, Bane thundered:

> America will "go over the top" in humanity's greatest battle [against liquor] and plant the victorious white standard of Prohibition upon the nation's loftiest eminence. Then catching sight of the beckoning hand of our sister nations across the sea, struggling with the same age-long foe, we will go forth with the spirit of the missionary and the crusader to help drive the demon of drink from all civilization. With America leading the way, with faith in Omnipotent God, and bearing with patriotic hands our stainless flag, the emblem of civic purity, we will soon bestow upon mankind the priceless gift of World Prohibition.[19]

Fortunately, the prohibitionists found the reluctant world a tougher nut to crack.

WOMEN AT WAR AND AT THE POLLS

Another direct outgrowth of World War I, coming in tandem with prohibition but lasting more permanently, was the Nineteenth Amendment, submitted by Congress in 1919 and ratified by the following year, which allowed women to vote. Women's

---

[19] Quoted in Timberlake, *Prohibition*, pp. 180–181.

suffrage had long been a movement directly allied with prohibition. Desperate to combat a demographic trend that seemed to be going against them, the evangelical pietists called for women's suffrage (and enacted it in many Western states). They did so because they knew that while pietist women were socially and politically active, ethnic or liturgical women tended to be culturally bound to hearth and home and therefore far less likely to vote. Hence, women's suffrage would greatly increase pietist voting power. In 1869 the Prohibitionist Party became the first party to endorse women's suffrage, which it continued to do. The Progressive Party was equally enthusiastic about female suffrage; it was the first major national party to permit women delegates at its conventions. A leading women's suffrage organization was the Women's Christian Temperance Union, which reached an enormous membership of 300,000 by 1900. And three successive presidents of the major women's suffrage group, the National American Woman Suffrage Association—Susan B. Anthony, Mrs. Carrie Chapman Catt, and Dr. Anna Howard Shaw—all began their activist careers as prohibitionists. Susan B. Anthony put the issue clearly:

> There is an enemy of the homes of this nation and that enemy is drunkenness. Everyone connected with the gambling house, the brothel and the saloon works and votes solidly against the enfranchisement of women, and, I say, if you believe in chastity, if you believe in honesty and integrity, then take the necessary steps to put the ballot in the hands of women.[20]

For its part, the German-American Alliance of Nebraska sent out an appeal during the unsuccessful referendum in November 1914 on women suffrage. Written in German, the appeal

[20] Quoted in Alan P. Grimes, *The Puritan Ethic and Woman Suffrage* (New York: Oxford University Press, 1967), p. 78.

declared, "Our German women do not want the right to vote, and since our opponents desire the right of suffrage mainly for the purpose of saddling the yoke of prohibition on our necks, we should oppose it with all our might. . . ."[21]

America's entry into World War I provided the impetus for overcoming the substantial opposition to woman suffrage, as a corollary to the success of prohibition and as a reward for the vigorous activity by organized women in behalf of the war effort. To close the loop, much of that activity consisted in stamping out vice and alcohol as well as instilling "patriotic" education into the minds of often suspect immigrant groups.

Shortly after the US declaration of war, the Council of National Defense created an Advisory Committee on Women's Defense Work, known as the Woman's Committee. The purpose of the committee, writes a celebratory contemporary account, was "to coordinate the activities and the resources of the organized and unorganized women of the country, that their power may be immediately utilized in time of need, and to supply a new and direct channel of cooperation between women and governmental department."[22] Chairman of the Woman's Committee, working energetically and full time, was the former president of the National American Woman Suffrage Association, Dr. Anna Howard Shaw, and another leading member was the suffrage group's current chairman and an equally prominent suffragette, Mrs. Carrie Chapman Catt.

The Woman's Committee promptly set up organizations in cities and states across the country, and on June 19, 1917 convened a conference of over fifty national women's organizations to coordinate their efforts. It was at this conference that "the first definite task was imposed upon American women" by the

---

[21] Grimes, *Puritan Ethic*, p. 116.

[22] Ida Clyde Clarke, *American Women and the World War* (New York: D. Appleton and Co., 1918), p. 19.

indefatigable Food Czar, Herbert Hoover.[23] Hoover enlisted the cooperation of the nation's women in his ambitious campaign for controlling, restricting, and cartelizing the food industry in the name of "conservation" and elimination of "waste." Celebrating this coming together of women was one of the Woman's Committee members, the Progressive writer and muckraker Mrs. Ida M. Tarbell. Mrs. Tarbell lauded the "growing consciousness everywhere that this great enterprise for democracy which we are launching [the US entry into the war] is a national affair, and if an individual or a society is going to do its bit it must act with and under the government at Washington." "Nothing else," Mrs. Tarbell gushed, "can explain the action of the women of the country in coming together as they are doing today under one centralized direction."[24]

Mrs. Tarbell's enthusiasm might have been heightened by the fact that she was one of the *directing* rather than the *directed*. Herbert Hoover came to the women's conference with the proposal that each of the women sign and distribute a "food pledge card" on behalf of food conservation. While support for the food pledge among the public was narrower than anticipated, educational efforts to promote the pledge became the basis of the remainder of the women's conservation campaign. The Woman's Committee appointed Mrs. Tarbell as chairman of its committee on Food Administration, and she not only tirelessly organized the campaign but also wrote many letters and newspaper and magazine articles on its behalf.

In addition to food control, another important and immediate function of the Woman's Committee was to attempt to

---

[23] Clarke, *American Women*, p. 27.

[24] Ibid., p. 31. Actually Mrs. Tarbell's muckraking activities were pretty much confined to Rockefeller and Standard Oil. She was highly favorable to business leaders in the Morgan ambit, as witness her laudatory biographies of Judge Elbert H. Gary, of US Steel (1925) and Owen D. Young of General Electric (1932).

register every woman in the country for possible volunteer or paid work in support of the war effort. Every woman aged sixteen or over was asked to sign and submit a registration card with all pertinent information, including training, experience, and the sort of work desired. In that way the government would know the whereabouts and training of every woman, and government and women could then serve each other best. In many states, especially Ohio and Illinois, state governments set up schools to train the registrars. And even though the Woman's Committee kept insisting that the registration was completely voluntary, the state of Louisiana, as Ida Clarke puts it, developed a "novel and clever" idea to facilitate the program: women's registration was made compulsory.

Louisiana's Governor Ruftin G. Pleasant decreed October 17, 1917 compulsory registration day, and a host of state officials collaborated in its operation. The State Food Commission made sure that food pledges were also signed by all, and the State School Board granted a holiday on October 17 so that teachers could assist in the compulsory registration, especially in the rural districts. Six thousand women were officially commissioned by the state of Louisiana to conduct the registration, and they worked in tandem with state Food Conservation officials and parish Demonstration Agents. In the French areas of the state, the Catholic priests rendered valuable aid in personally appealing to all their female parishioners to perform their registration duties. Handbills were circulated in French, house-to-house canvasses were made, and speeches urging registration were made by women activists in movie theaters, schools, churches, and courthouses. We are informed that all responses were eager and cordial; there is no mention of any resistance. We are also advised that "even the negroes were quite alive to the situation, meeting sometimes with the white people and sometimes at the call of their own pastors."[25]

---

[25] Ibid., p. 277, pp. 275–79, p. 58.

Also helping out in women's registration and food control was another, smaller, but slightly more sinister women's organization that had been launched by Congress as a sort of prewar wartime group at a large Congress for Constructive Patriotism, held in Washington, D.C. in late January 1917. This was the National League for Woman's Service (NLWS), which established a nationwide organization later overshadowed and overlapped by the larger Woman's Committee. The difference was that the NLWS was set up on quite frankly military lines. Each local working unit was called a "detachment" under a "detachment commander," district-wide and state-wide detachments met in annual "encampments," and every woman member was to wear a uniform with an organization badge and insignia. In particular, "the basis of training for all detachments is standardized, physical drill."[26]

A vital part of the Woman's Committee work was engaging in "patriotic education." The government and the Woman's Committee recognized that immigrant ethnic women were most in need of such vital instruction, and so it set up a committee on education, headed by the energetic Mrs. Carrie Chapman Catt. Mrs. Catt stated the problem well to the Woman's Committee: Millions of people in the United States were unclear on why we were at war, and why, as Ida Clarke paraphrases Mrs. Catt there is "the imperative necessity of winning the war if future generations were to be protected from the menace of an unscrupulous militarism."[27] Presumably US militarism, being "scrupulous," posed no problem.

Apathy and ignorance abounded, Mrs. Catt went on, and she proposed to mobilize twenty million American women, the "greatest sentiment makers of any community," to begin a "vast educational movement" to get the women "fervently enlisted to

[26] Ibid., p. 183.

[27] Ibid., p. 103.

push the war to victory as rapidly as possible." As Mrs. Catt continued, however, the clarity of war aims she called for really amounted to pointing out that we were in the war "whether the nation likes it or does not like it," and that therefore the "sacrifices" needed to win the war "willingly or unwillingly must be made." In the end, Mrs. Catt could come up with only one reasoned argument for the war, apart from this alleged necessity, that it must be won to make it "the war to end war."[28]

The "patriotic education" campaign of the organized women was largely to "Americanize" immigrant women by energetically persuading them (a) to become naturalized American citizens and (b) to learn "Mother English." In the campaign, dubbed "America First," national unity was promoted through getting immigrants to learn English and trying to get female immigrants into afternoon or evening English classes. The organized patriot women were also worried about preserving the family structure of the immigrants. If the children learn English and their parents remain ignorant, children will scorn their elders, "parental discipline and control are dissipated, and the whole family fabric becomes weakened. Thus one of the great conservative forces in the community becomes inoperative." To preserve "maternal control of the young," then, "Americanization of the foreign women through language becomes imperative." In Erie, Pennsylvania, women's clubs appointed "Block Matrons," whose job it was to get to know the foreign families of the neighborhood and to back up school authorities in urging the immigrants to learn English, and who, in the rather naive words of Ida Clarke, "become neighbors, friends, and veritable mother confessors to the foreign women of the block." One would like to have heard some comments from recipients of the attentions of the Block Matrons.

[28] Ibid., pp. 104–05.

All in all, as a result of the Americanization campaign, Ida Clarke concludes, "the organized women of this country can play an important part in making ours a country with a common language, a common purpose, a common set of ideals—a unified America."[29]

Neither did the government and its organized women neglect progressive economic reforms. At the organizing June 1917 conference of the Woman's Committee, Mrs. Carrie Catt emphasized that the greatest problem of the war was to assure that women receive "equal pay for equal work." The conference suggested that vigilance committees be established to guard against the violation of "ethical laws" governing labor and also that all laws restricting ("protecting") the labor of women and children be rigorously enforced. Apparently, there were some values to which maximizing production for the war effort had to take second place.

Mrs. Margaret Dreier Robins, president of the National Women's Trade Union's League, hailed the fact that the Woman's Committee was organizing committees in every state to protect minimum standards for women and children's labor in industry and demanded minimum wages and shorter hours for women. Mrs. Robins particularly warned that "not only are unorganized women workers in vast numbers used as underbidders in the labor market for lowering industrial standards, but they are related to those groups in industrial centers of our country that are least Americanized and most alien to our institutions and ideals." And so "Americanization" and cartelization of female labor went hand in hand.[30]

---

[29] Ibid., p. 101.

[30] Ibid., p. 129. Margaret Dreier Robins and her husband Raymond were virtually a paradigmatic progressive couple. Raymond was a Florida-born wanderer and successful gold prospector who underwent a mystical conversion experience in the Alaska wilds and became a pietist preacher. He moved to Chicago, where he became a leader in Chicago settlement house work and

SAVING OUR BOYS FROM ALCOHOL AND VICE

One of organized womanhood's major contributions to the war effort was to collaborate in an attempt to save American soldiers from vice and Demon Rum. In addition to establishing rigorous dry zones around every military camp in the United States, the Selective Service Act of May 1917 also outlawed prostitution in wide zones around the military camps. To enforce these provisions, the War Department had ready at hand a Commission on Training Camp Activities, an agency soon imitated by the Department of the Navy. Both commissions were headed by a man tailor-made for the job, the progressive New York settlement-house worker, municipal political reformer, and former student and disciple of Woodrow Wilson, Raymond Blaine Fosdick.

---

municipal reform. Margaret Dreier and her sister Mary were daughters of a wealthy and socially prominent New York family who worked for and financed the emergent National Women's Trade Union League. Margaret married Raymond Robins in 1905 and moved to Chicago, soon becoming longtime president of the league. In Chicago, the Robinses led and organized progressive political causes for over two decades, becoming top leaders of the Progressive Party from 1912 to 1916. During the war, Raymond Robins engaged in considerable diplomatic activity as head of a Red Cross mission to Russia. On the Robinses, see Allen F. Davis, *Spearhead for Reform: The Social Settlements and the Progressive Movement, 1890–1914* (New York: Oxford University Press, 1967).

For more on women's war work and woman suffrage, see the standard history of the suffrage movement, Eleanor Flexner, *Century of Struggle: The Woman's Rights Movement in the United States* (New York: Atheneum, 1968), pp. 288–89. Interestingly, The National War Labor Board (NWLB) frankly adopted the concept of "equal pay for equal work in order to limit the employment of women workers by imposing higher costs on the employer. The "only check," affirmed the NWLB, on excessive employment of women "is to make it no more profitable to employ women than men." Quoted in Valerie I. Conner, "'The Mothers of the Race' in World War I: The National War Labor Board and Women in Industry," *Labor History* 21 (Winter, 1979–80): 34.

Fosdick's background, life, and career were paradigmatic for progressive intellectuals and activists of that era. Fosdick's ancestors were Yankees from Massachusetts and Connecticut, and his great-grandfather pioneered westward in a covered wagon to become a frontier farmer in the heart of the Burned-Over District of transplanted Yankees, Buffalo, New York. Fosdick's grandfather, a pietist lay preacher born again in a Baptist revival, was a prohibitionist who married a preacher's daughter and became a lifelong public school teacher in Buffalo. Grandfather Fosdick rose to become Superintendent of Education in Buffalo and a battler for an expanded and strengthened public school system.

Fosdick's immediate ancestry continued in the same vein. His father was a public school teacher in Buffalo who rose to become principal of a high school. His mother was deeply pietist and a staunch advocate of prohibition and women's suffrage. Fosdick's father was a devout pietist Protestant and a "fanatical" Republican who gave his son Raymond the middle name of his hero, the veteran Maine Republican James G. Blaine. The three Fosdick children, elder brother Harry Emerson, Raymond, and Raymond's twin sister, Edith, on emerging from this atmosphere, all forged lifetime careers of pietism and social service.

While active in New York reform administration, Fosdick made a fateful friendship. In 1910, John D. Rockefeller, Jr., like his father a pietist Baptist, was chairman of a special grand jury to investigate and to try to stamp out prostitution in New York City. For Rockefeller, the elimination of prostitution was to become an ardent and lifelong crusade. He believed that sin, such as prostitution, must be criminated, quarantined, and driven underground through rigorous suppression.

In 1911, Rockefeller began his crusade by setting up the Bureau of Social Hygiene, into which he poured $5 million in the next quarter century. Two years later he enlisted Fosdick, already a speaker at the annual dinner of Rockefeller's Baptist

Bible class, to study police systems in Europe in conjunction with activities to end the great "social vice." Surveying American police after his stint in Europe at Rockefeller's behest, Fosdick was appalled that police work in the United States was not considered a "science" and that it was subject to "sordid" political influences.[31]

At that point, the new Secretary of War, the progressive former mayor of Cleveland Newton D. Baker, became disturbed at reports that areas near the army camps in Texas on the Mexican border, where troops were mobilized to combat the Mexican revolutionary Pancho Villa, were honeycombed with saloons and prostitution. Sent by Baker on a fact-finding tour in the summer of 1916, scoffed at by tough army officers as the "Reverend," Fosdick was horrified to find saloons and brothels seemingly everywhere in the vicinity of the military camps. He reported his consternation to Baker, and, at Fosdick's suggestion, Baker cracked down on the army commanders and their lax attitude toward alcohol and vice. But Fosdick was beginning to get the glimmer of another idea. Couldn't the suppression of the bad be accompanied by a positive encouragement of the good, of wholesome recreational alternatives to sin and liquor that our boys could enjoy? When war was declared, Baker quickly appointed Fosdick to be chairman of the Commission on Training Camp Activities.

Armed with the coercive resources of the federal government and rapidly building his bureaucratic empire from merely one secretary to a staff of thousands, Raymond Fosdick set out with determination on his twofold task: stamping out alcohol

---

[31] See Raymond B. Fosdick, *Chronicle of a Generation: An Autobiography* (New York: Harper & Bros., 1958), p. 133. Also see Peter Collier and David Horowitz, *The Rockefellers: An American Dynasty* (New York: New American Library, 1976), pp. 103–05. Fosdick was particularly appalled that American patrolmen on street duty actually smoked cigars! Fosdick, *Chronicle*, p. 135.

and sin in and around every military camp, and filling the void for American soldiers and sailors by providing them with wholesome recreation. As head of the Law Enforcement Division of the Training Camp Commission, Fosdick selected Bascom Johnson, attorney for the American Social Hygiene Association.[32] Johnson was commissioned a major, and his staff of forty aggressive attorneys became second lieutenants.

---

[32] The American Social Hygiene Association, with its influential journal *Social Hygiene*, was the major organization in what was known as the "purity crusade." The association was launched when the New York physician Dr. Prince A. Marrow, inspired by the agitation against venereal disease and in favor of the continence urged by the French syphilographer, Jean-Alfred Fournier, formed in 1905 the American Society for Sanitary and Moral Prophylaxis (ASSMP). Soon, the terms proposed by the Chicago branch of ASSMP, "social hygiene" and "sex hygiene," became widely used for their medical and scientific patina, and in 1910 ASSMP changed its name to the American Federation for Sex Hygiene (AFSH). Finally, in late 1913, AFSH, an organization of physicians, combined with the National Vigilance Association (formerly the American Purity Alliance), a group of clergymen and social workers, to form the all-embracing American Social Hygiene Association (ASHA).

In this social hygiene movement, the moral and medical went hand in hand. Thus Dr. Morrow welcomed the new knowledge about venereal disease because it demonstrated that "punishment for sexual sin" no longer had to be "reserved for the hereafter."

The first president of ASHA was the president of Harvard University, Charles W. Eliot. In his address to the first meeting, Eliot made clear that total abstinence from alcohol, tobacco, and even spices was part and parcel of the anti-prostitution and purity crusade.

On physicians, the purity crusade, and the formation of ASHA, see Ronald Hamowy, "Medicine and the Crimination of Sin: 'Self-Abuse' in 19th Century America," The *Journal of Libertarian Studies* I (Summer, 1972): 247–59; James Wunsch, "Prostitution and Public Policy: From Regulation to Suppression, 1858–1920," Ph.D. diss., University of Chicago, 1976; and Roland R. Wagner, "Virtue Against Vice: A Study of Moral Reformers and Prostitution in the Progressive Era," Ph.D. diss., University of Wisconsin, 1971. On Morrow, also see John C. Burnham. "The Progressive Era

Employing the argument of health and military necessity, Fosdick set up a Social Hygiene Division of his commission, which promulgated the slogan "Fit to Fight." Using a mixture of force and threats to remove federal troops from the bases if recalcitrant cities did not comply, Fosdick managed to bludgeon his way into suppressing, if not prostitution in general, then at least every major red light district in the country. In doing so, Fosdick and Baker, employing local police and the federal Military Police, far exceeded their legal authority. The law authorized the president to shut down every red light district in a five-mile zone around each military camp or base. Of the 110 red light districts shut down by military force, however, only 35 were included in the prohibited zone. Suppression of the other 75 was an illegal extension of the law. Nevertheless, Fosdick was triumphant: "Through the efforts of this Commission [on Training Camp Activities] the red light district has practically ceased to be a feature of American city life."[33] The result of this permanent destruction of the red light district, of course, was to drive prostitution onto the streets, where consumers would be deprived of the protection of either an open market or of regulation.

In some cases, the federal anti-vice crusade met considerable resistance. Secretary of Navy Josephus Daniels, a progressive from North Carolina, had to call out the marines to patrol

---

Revolution in American Attitudes Toward Sex," *Journal of American History* 59 (March 1973) 899, and Paul Boyer, *Urban Masses and Moral Order in America, 1820–1920* (Cambridge, Mass.: Harvard University Press, 1978), p. 201. Also see Burnham, "Medical Specialists and Movements Toward Social Control in the Progressive Era: Three Examples," in J. Israel, ed., *Building the Organizational Society: Essays in Associational Activities in Modern America* (New York: Free Press, 1972), pp. 24–26.

[33] In Daniel R. Beaver, *Newton D. Baker and the American War Effort 1917–1919* (Lincoln: University of Nebraska Press, 1966), p. 222. Also see ibid., pp. 221–24; and C.H. Cramer, *Newton D. Baker: A Biography* (Cleveland: World Publishing Co., 1961), pp. 99–102.

the streets of resistant Philadelphia, and naval troops, over the strenuous objections of the mayor, were used to crush the fabled red light district of Storyville, in New Orleans, in November 1917.[34]

In its hubris, the US Army decided to extend its anti-vice crusade to foreign shores. General John J. Pershing issued an official bulletin to members of the American Expeditionary Force in France urging that "sexual continence is the plain duty of members of the A.E.F., both for the vigorous conduct of the war, and for the clean health of the American people after the war." Pershing and the American military tried to close all the French brothels in areas where American troops were located, but the move was unsuccessful because the French objected bitterly. Premier Georges Clemenceau pointed out that the result of the "total prohibition of regulated prostitution in the vicinity of American troops" was only to increase "venereal diseases among the civilian population of the neighborhood." Finally, the United States had to rest content with declaring French civilian areas off limits to the troops.[35]

The more positive part of Raymond Fosdick's task during the war was supplying the soldiers and sailors with a constructive substitute for sin and alcohol, "healthful amusements and

---

[34] Fosdick, *Chronicle*, pp. 145–47. While prostitution was indeed banned in Storyville after 1917, Storyville, contrary to legend, never "closed"—the saloons and dance halls remained open, and contrary to orthodox accounts, jazz was never really shut down in Storyville or New Orleans, and it was therefore never forced up river. For a revisionist view of the impact of the closure of Storyville on the history of jazz, see Tom Bethell, *George Lewis: A Jazzman from New Orleans* (Berkeley: University of California Press, 1977), pp. 6–7; and Al Rose, *Storyville, New Orleans* (Montgomery: University of Alabama Press, 1974). Also, on later Storyville, see Boyer, *Urban Masses*, p. 218.

[35] See Hamowy, "Crimination of Sin," p. 226 *n*. The quote from Clemenceau is in Fosdick, *Chronicle*, p. 171. Newton Baker's loyal biographer declared that Clemenceau, in this response, showed "his animal proclivities as the 'Tiger of France.'" Cramer, *Newton Baker*, p. 101.

wholesome company." As might be expected, the Woman's Committee and organized womanhood collaborated enthusiastically. They followed the injunction of Secretary of War Baker that the government "cannot allow these young men to be surrounded by a vicious and demoralizing environment, nor can we leave anything undone which will protect them from unhealthy influences and crude forms of temptation." The Woman's Committee found, however, that in the great undertaking of safeguarding the health and morals of our boys, their most challenging problem proved to be guarding the morals of their mobilized young girls. For unfortunately, "where soldiers are stationed the problem of preventing girls from being misled by the glamour and romance of war and beguiling uniforms looms large." Fortunately, perhaps, the Maryland Committee proposed the establishment of a "Patriotic League of Honor which will inspire girls to adopt the highest standards of womanliness and loyalty to their country."[36]

No group was more delighted with the achievements of Fosdick and his Military Training Camp Commission than the burgeoning profession of social work. Surrounded by handpicked aides from the Playground and Recreation Association and the Russell Sage Foundation, Fosdick and the others "in effect tried to create a massive settlement house around each camp. No army had ever seen anything like it before, but it was an outgrowth of the recreation and community organization movement, and a victory for those who had been arguing for

[36] Clarke, *American Women*, pp. 90, 87, 93. In some cases, organized women took the offensive to help stamp out vice and liquor in their community. Thus in Texas in 1917 the Texas Women's Anti-Vice Committee led in the creation of a "White Zone" around all the military bases. By autumn the Committee expanded into the Texas Social Hygiene Association to coordinate the work of eradicating prostitution and saloons. San Antonio proved to be its biggest problem. Lewis L. Gould, *Progressives and Prohibitionists: Texas Democrats in the Wilson Era* (Austin: University of Texas Press, 1973), p. 227.

the creative use of leisure time."[37] The social work profession pronounced the program an enormous success. The influential *Survey* magazine summed up the result as "the most stupendous piece of social work in modern times."[38]

Social workers were also exultant about prohibition. In 1917, the National Conference of Charities and Corrections (which changed its name around the same time to the National Conference of Social Work) was emboldened to drop whatever value-free pose it might have had and come out squarely for prohibition. On returning from Russia in 1917, Edward T. Devine of the Charity Organization Society of New York exclaimed that "the social revolution which followed the prohibition of vodka was more profoundly important than the political revolution which abolished autocracy." And Robert A. Woods of Boston, the Grand Old Man of the settlement house movement and a veteran advocate of prohibition, predicted in 1919 that the Eighteenth Amendment, "one of the greatest and best events in history," would reduce poverty, wipe out prostitution and crime, and liberate "vast suppressed human potentialities."[39]

---

[37] Davis, *Spearheads for Reform*, p. 225.

[38] Fosdick, *Chronicle*, p. 144. After the war, Raymond Fosdick went on to fame and fortune, first as Under Secretary General of the League of Nations, and then for the rest of his life as a member of the small inner circle close to John D. Rockefeller, Jr. In that capacity, Fosdick rose to become head of the Rockefeller Foundation and Rockefeller's official biographer. Meanwhile, Fosdick's brother, Rev. Harry Emerson, became Rockefeller's hand-picked parish minister, first at Park Avenue Presbyterian Church and then at the new interdenominational Riverside Church, built with Rockefeller funds. Harry Emerson Fosdick was Rockefeller's principal aide in battling, within the Protestant Church, in favor of postmillennial, statist, "liberal" Protestantism and against the rising tide of premillennial Christianity, known as "fundamentalist" since the years before World War I. See Collier and Horowitz, *The Rockefellers*, pp. 140–42, 151–53.

[39] Davis, *Spearheads for Reform*, p. 226; Timberlake, *Prohibition*, p. 66; Boyer, *Urban Masses*, p. 156.

Woods, president of the National Conference of Social Work during 1917–18, had long denounced alcohol as "an abominable evil." A postmillennial pietist, he believed in "Christian statesmanship" that would, in "propaganda of the deed," Christianize the social order in a corporate, communal route to the glorification of God. Like many pietists, Woods cared not for creeds or dogmas but only for advancing Christianity in a communal way; though an active Episcopalian, his "parish" was the community at large. In his settlement work, Woods had long favored the isolation or segregation of the "unfit," in particular "the tramp, the drunkard, the pauper, the imbecile," with the settlement house as the nucleus of this reform. Woods was particularly eager to isolate and punish the drunkard and the tramp. "Inveterate drunkards" were to receive increasing levels of "punishment," with ever-lengthier jail terms. The "tramp evil" was to be gotten rid of by rounding up and jailing vagrants, who would be placed in tramp workhouses and put to forced labor.

For Woods the world war was a momentous event. It had advanced the process of "Americanization," a "great humanizing process through which all loyalties, all beliefs must be wrought together in a better order."[40] The war had wonderfully released the energies of the American people. Now, however, it was important to carry the wartime momentum into the postwar world. Lauding the war collectivist society during the spring of 1918, Robert Woods asked the crucial question, "Why should it not always be so? Why not continue in the years of peace this close, vast, wholesome organism of service, of fellowship, of constructive creative power?"[41]

---

[40] Eleanor H. Woods, *Robert A. Woods; Champion of Democracy* (Boston: Houghton Mifflin, 1929), p. 316. Also see ibid., pp. 201–02, 250ff., 268ff.

[41] Davis, *Spearheads for Reform*, p. 227.

THE *NEW REPUBLIC* COLLECTIVISTS

The *New Republic* magazine, founded in 1914 as the leading intellectual organ of progressivism, was a living embodiment of the burgeoning alliance between big-business interests, in particular the House of Morgan, and the growing legion of collectivist intellectuals. Founder and publisher of the *New Republic* was Willard W. Straight, partner of J.P. Morgan & Co., and its financier was Straight's wife, the heiress Dorothy Whitney. Major editor of the influential new weekly was the veteran collectivist and theoretician of Teddy Roosevelt's New Nationalism, Herbert David Croly. Croly's two coeditors were Walter Edward Weyl, another theoretician of the New Nationalism, and the young, ambitious former official of the Intercollegiate Socialist Society, the future pundit Walter Lippmann. As Woodrow Wilson began to take America into World War I, the *New Republic*, though originally Rooseveltian, became an enthusiastic supporter of the war, and a virtual spokesman for the Wilson war effort, the wartime collectivist economy, and the new society molded by the war.

On the higher levels of ratiocination, unquestionably the leading progressive intellectual, before, during, and after World War I, was the champion of pragmatism, Professor John Dewey of Columbia University. Dewey wrote frequently for the *New Republic* in this period and was clearly its leading theoretician. A Yankee born in 1859, Dewey was, as Mencken put it, "of indestructible Vermont stock and a man of the highest bearable sobriety." John Dewey was the son of a small town Vermont grocer.[42] Although he was a pragmatist and a secular humanist most of his life, it is not as well known that Dewey, in the years before 1900, was a postmillennial pietist, seeking the gradual development of a Christianized social order and Kingdom of

---

[42] H.L. Mencken, "Professor Veblen," in *A Mencken Chrestomathy* (New York: Alfred A. Knopf, 1949), p. 267.

God on earth via the expansion of science, community, and the State. During the 1890s, Dewey, as professor of philosophy at the University of Michigan, expounded his vision of postmillennial pietism in a series of lectures before the Students' Christian Association. Dewey argued that the growth of modem science now makes it possible for man to establish the biblical idea of the Kingdom of God on earth. Once humans had broken free of the restraints of orthodox Christianity, a truly religious Kingdom of God could be realized in "the common incarnate Life, the purpose animating all men and binding them together into one harmonious whole of sympathy."[43]

Religion would thus work in tandem with science and democracy, all of which would break down the barriers between men and establish the Kingdom. After 1900 it was easy for John Dewey, along with most other postmillennial intellectuals of the period, to shift gradually but decisively from postmillennial progressive Christian statism to progressive secular statism. The path, the expansion of statism and "social control" and planning, remained the same. And even though the Christian creed dropped out of the picture, the intellectuals and activists continued to possess the same evangelical zeal for the salvation of the world that their parents and they themselves had once possessed. The world would and must still be saved through progress and statism.[44]

---

[43] Quoted in the important article by Jean B. Quandt, "Religion and Social Thought: The Secularization of Postmillennialism," *American Quarterly* 25 (October 1973): 404. Also see John Blewett, S.J., "Democracy as Religion: Unity in Human Relations," in Blewett, ed., *John Dewey: His Thought and Influence* (New York: Fordham University Press, 1960), pp. 33–58; and *John Dewey: The Early Works, 1882–1989*, eds., J. Boydstan et al. (Carbondale: Southern Illinois University Press, 1969–71), vols. 2 and 3.

[44] On the general secularization of postmillennial pietism after 1900, see Quandt, "Religion and Social Thought," pp. 390–409; and James H. Moorhead, "The Erosion of Postmillennialism in American Religious Thought, 1865–1925," *Church History* 53 (March 1984): 61–77.

A pacifist while in the midst of peace, John Dewey prepared himself to lead the parade for war as America drew nearer to armed intervention in the European struggle. First, in January 1916 in the *New Republic*, Dewey attacked the "professional pacifist's" outright condemnation of war as a "sentimental phantasy," a confusion of means and ends. Force, he declared, was simply "a means of getting results," and therefore would neither be lauded or condemned per se. Next, in April Dewey signed a pro-Allied manifesto, not only cheering for an Allied victory but also proclaiming that the Allies were "struggling to preserve the liberties of the world and the highest ideals of civilization." And though Dewey supported US entry into the war so that Germany could be defeated, "a hard job, but one which had to be done," he was far more interested in the wonderful changes that the war would surely bring about in the domestic American polity. In particular, war offered a golden opportunity to bring about collectivist social control in the interest of social justice. As one historian put it,

> because war demanded paramount commitment to the national interest and necessitated an unprecedented degree of government planning and economic regulation in that interest, Dewey saw the prospect of permanent socialization, permanent replacement of private and possessive interest by public and social interest, both within and among nations.[45]

In an interview with the *New York World* a few months after US entry into the war, Dewey exulted that "this war may easily be the beginning of the end of business." For out of the needs of the war, "we are beginning to produce for use, not for sale, and the capitalist is not a capitalist [in the face of] the war." Capitalist conditions of production and sale are now under gov-

---

[45] Carol S. Gruber, *Mars and Minerva: World War I and the Uses of the Higher Learning in America* (Baton Rouge: Louisiana State University Press, 1975), p. 92.

ernment control, and "there is no reason to believe that the old principle will ever be resumed.... Private property had already lost its sanctity . . . industrial democracy is on the way."[46]

In short, intelligence is at last being used to tackle social problems, and this practice is destroying the old order and creating a new social order of "democratic integrated control." Labor is acquiring more power, science is at last being socially mobilized, and massive government controls are socializing industry. These developments, Dewey proclaimed, were precisely what we are fighting for.[47]

Furthermore, John Dewey saw great possibilities opened by the war for the advent of worldwide collectivism. To Dewey, America's entrance into the war created a "plastic juncture" in the world, a world marked by a "world organization and the beginnings of a public control which crosses nationalistic boundaries and interests," and which would also "outlaw war."[48]

The editors of the *New Republic* took a position similar to Dewey's, except that they arrived at it even earlier. In his editorial in the magazine's first issue in November 1914, Herbert Croly cheerily prophesied that the war would stimulate America's spirit of nationalism and therefore bring it closer to

---

[46] Quoted in Gruber, *Mars and Minerva*, pp. 92–93. Also see William E. Leuchtenburg, "The New Deal and the Analogue of War," in J. Braeman, R. Bremner, and E. Walters, eds., *Change and Continuity in Twentieth-Century America* (New York: Harper & Row, 1966), p. 89. For similar reasons, Thorstein Veblen, prophet of the alleged dichotomy of production for profit vs. production for use, championed the war and began to come out openly for socialism in an article in the *New Republic* in 1918, later reprinted in his *The Vested Interests and the State of the Industrial Arts* (1919). See Charles Hirschfeld, "Nationalist Progressivism and World War I," *Mid-America* 45 (July 1963), p. 150. Also see David Riesman, *Thorstein Veblen: A Critical Interpretation* (New York: Charles Scribner's Sons, 1960), pp. 30–31.

[47] Hirschfeld, "Nationalist Progressivism," p. 150.

[48] Gruber, *Mars and Minerva*, p. 92.

democracy. At first hesitant about the collectivist war economies in Europe, the *New Republic* soon began to cheer and urged the United States to follow the lead of the warring European nations and socialize its economy and expand the powers of the State.

As America prepared to enter the war, the *New Republic*, examining war collectivism in Europe, rejoiced that "on its administrative side socialism [had] won a victory that [was] superb and compelling." True, European war collectivism was a bit grim and autocratic, but never fear, America could use the selfsame means for "democratic" goals.

The *New Republic* intellectuals also delighted in the "war spirit" in America, for that spirit meant "the substitution of national and social and organic forces for the more or less mechanical private forces operative in peace." The purposes of war and social reform might be a bit different, but, after all, "they are both purposes, and luckily for mankind a social organization which is efficient is as useful for the one as for the other."[49] Lucky indeed.

As America prepared to enter the war, the *New Republic* eagerly looked forward to imminent collectivization, sure that it would bring "immense gains in national efficiency and happiness." After war was declared, the magazine urged that the war be used as "an aggressive tool of democracy." "Why should not the war serve," the magazine asked, "as a pretext to be used to foist innovations upon the country?" In that way, progressive intellectuals could lead the way in abolishing "the typical evils of the sprawling half-educated competitive capitalism."

Convinced that the United States would attain socialism through war, Walter Lippmann, in a public address shortly

---

[49] Hirschfeld, "Nationalist Progressivism," p. 142. It is intriguing that for the *New Republic*, intellectuals, actually existent private individuals are dismissed as "mechanical," whereas nonexistent entities such as "national and social" forces are hailed as being "organic."

after American entry, trumpeted his apocalyptic vision of the future:

> We who have gone to war to insure democracy in the world will have raised an aspiration here that will not end with the overthrow of the Prussian autocracy. We shall turn with fresh interests to our own tyrannies—to our Colorado mines, our autocratic steel industries, sweatshops, and our slums. A force is loose in America. Our own reactionaries will not assuage it. We shall know how to deal with them.[50]

Walter Lippmann, indeed, had been the foremost hawk among the *New Republic* intellectuals. He had pushed Croly into backing Wilson and into supporting intervention, and then had collaborated with Colonel House in pushing Wilson into entering the war. Soon Lippmann, an enthusiast for conscription, had to confront the fact that he himself, only twenty-seven years old and in fine health, was eminently eligible for the

---

[50] Quoted in Hirschfeld, "Nationalist Progressivism," p. 147. A minority of pro-war Socialists broke off from the antiwar Socialist Party to form the Social Democratic League, and to join a pro-war front organized and financed by the Wilson administration, the American Alliance for Labor and Democracy. The pro-war socialists welcomed the war as providing "startling progress in collectivism," and opined that after the war, the existent state socialism would be advanced toward "democratic collectivism." The pro-war socialists included John Spargo, Algie Simons, W.J. Ghent, Robert R. LaMonte, Charles Edward Russell, J.G. Phelps Stokes, Upton Sinclair, and William English Walling. Walling so succumbed to war fever that he denounced the Socialist Party as a conscious tool of the Kaiser and advocated the suppression of freedom of speech for pacifists and for antiwar socialists. See Hirschfeld, "Nationalist Progressivism," p. 143. On Walling, see James Gilbert, *Designing the Industrial State: The Intellectual Pursuit of Collectivism in America, 1880–1940* (Chicago: Quadrangle Books, 1972), pp. 232–33. On the American Alliance for Labor and Democracy and its role in the war effort, see Ronald Radosh, *American Labor and United States Foreign Policy* (New York: Random House, 1969), pp. 58–71.

draft. Somehow, however, Lippmann failed to unite theory and praxis.

Young Felix Frankfurter, progressive Harvard Law Professor and a close associate of the *New Republic* editorial staff, had just been selected as a special assistant to Secretary of War Baker. Lippmann somehow felt that his own inestimable services could be better used planning the postwar world than battling in the trenches. And so he wrote to Frankfurter asking for a job in Baker's office. "What I want to do," he pleaded, "is to devote all my time to studying and speculating on the approaches to peace and the reaction from the peace. Do you think you can get me an exemption on such highfalutin grounds?" He then rushed to reassure Frankfurter that there was nothing "personal" in this request. After all, he explained, "the things that need to be thought out, are so big that there must be no personal element mixed up with this." Frankfurter having paved the way, Lippmann wrote to Secretary Baker. He assured Baker that he was only applying for a job and draft exemption on the pleading of others and in stern submission to the national interest. As Lippmann put it in a remarkable demonstration of cant:

> I have consulted all the people whose advice I value and they urge me to apply for exemption. You can well understand that this is not a pleasant thing to do, and yet, after searching my soul as candidly as I know how, I am convinced that I can serve my bit much more effectively than as a private in the new armies.

No doubt.

As icing on the cake, Lippmann added an important bit of "disinformation." For, he piteously wrote to Baker, the fact is "that my father is dying and my mother is absolutely alone in the world. She does not know what his condition is, and I cannot tell anyone for fear it would become known." Apparently, no one else "knew" his father's condition either, including his father and the medical profession, for the elder Lippmann managed to peg along successfully for the next ten years.[51]

Secure in his draft exemption, Walter Lippmann hied off in high excitement to Washington, there to help run the war and, a few months later, to help direct Colonel House's secret conclave of historians and social scientists setting out to plan the shape of the future peace treaty and the postwar world. Let others fight and die in the trenches; Walter Lippmann had the satisfaction of knowing that his talents, at least, would be put to their best use by the newly emerging collectivist State.

As the war went on, Croly and the other editors, having lost Lippmann to the great world beyond, cheered every new development of the massively controlled war economy. The nationalization of railroads and shipping, the priorities and allocation system, the total domination of all parts of the food industry achieved by Herbert Hoover and the Food Administration, the pro-union policy, the high taxes, and the draft were all hailed by the *New Republic* as an expansion of democracy's power to plan for the general good. As the Armistice ushered in the postwar world, the *New Republic* looked back on the handiwork of the war and found it good: "We revolutionized our society." All that remained was to organize a new constitutional convention to complete the job of reconstructing America.[52]

---

[51] In fact, Jacob Lippmann was to contract cancer in 1925 and die two years later. Moreover, Lippmann, before and after Jacob's death, was supremely indifferent to his father. Ronald Steel, *Walter Lippman and the American Century* (New York: Random House, 1981), p. 5, pp. 116–17. On Walter Lippmann's enthusiasm for conscription, at least for others, see Beaver, *Newton Baker*, pp. 26–27.

[52] Hirschfeld, "Nationalist Progressivism," pp. 148–50. On the *New Republic* and the war, and particularly on John Dewey, also see Christopher Lasch, *The New Radicalism in America, 1889–1963: The Intellectual as a Social Type* (New York: Vintage Books, 1965), pp. 181–224, especially pp. 202–04. On the three *New Republic* editors, see Charles Forcey, *The Crossroads of Liberalism: Croly, Weyl, Lippmann and the Progressive Era, 1900–1925*

But the revolution had not been fully completed. Despite the objections of Bernard Baruch and other wartime planners, the government decided not to make most of the war collectivist machinery permanent. From then on, the fondest ambition of Baruch and the others was to make the World War I system a permanent institution of American life. The most trenchant epitaph on the World War I polity was delivered by Rexford Guy Tugwell, the most frankly collectivist of the Brain Trusters of Franklin Roosevelt's New Deal. Looking back on "America's wartime socialism" in 1927, Tugwell lamented that if only the war had lasted longer, that great "experiment" could have been completed: "We were on the verge of having an international industrial machine when peace broke," Tugwell mourned. "Only the Armistice prevented a great experiment in control of production, control of prices, and control of consumption."[53] Tugwell need not have been troubled; there would soon be other emergencies, other wars.

At the end of the war, Lippmann was to go on to become America's foremost journalistic pundit. Croly, having broken with the Wilson Administration on the harshness of the Versailles Treaty, was bereft to find the *New Republic* no longer the spokesman for some great political leader. During the late 1920s he was to discover an exemplary national collectivist leader abroad—in Benito Mussolini.[54] That Croly ended his

(New York: Oxford University Press, 1961). Also see David W. Noble, "The *New Republic* and the Idea of Progress, 1914–1920," *Mississippi Valley Historical Review* 38 (December 1951): 387–402. In a book titled *The End of the War* (1918), *New Republic* editor Walter Weyl assured his readers that "the new economic solidarity once gained, can never again be surrendered." Cited in Leuchtenburg. "New Deal," p. 90.

[53] Rexford Guy Tugwell, "America's War-Time Socialism" *The Nation* (1927), pp. 364–65. Quoted in Leuchtenburg, "The New Deal," pp. 90–91.

[54] In January 1927, Croly wrote a *New Republic* editorial, "An Apology for Fascism," endorsing an accompanying article, "Fascism for the Italians," written

years as an admirer of Mussolini comes as no surprise when we realize that from early childhood he had been steeped by a doting father in the authoritarian socialist doctrines of Auguste Comte's Positivism. These views were to mark Croly throughout his life. Thus, Herbert's father, David, the founder of Positivism in the United States, advocated the establishment of vast powers of government over everyone's life. David Croly favored the growth of trusts and monopolies as a means both to that end and also to eliminate the evils of individual competition and "selfishness." Like his son, David Croly railed at the Jeffersonian "fear of government" in America, and looked to Hamilton as an example to counter that trend.[55]

---

by the distinguished philosopher Horace M. Kallen, a disciple of John Dewey and an exponent of progressive pragmatism. Kallen praised Mussolini for his pragmatic approach, and in particular for the *élan vital* that Mussolini had infused into Italian life. True, Professor Kallen conceded, fascism is coercive, but surely this is only a temporary expedient. Noting fascism's excellent achievement in economics, education, and administrative reform, Kallen added that "in this respect the Fascist revolution is not unlike the Communist revolution. Each is the application by force . . . of an ideology to a condition. Each should have the freest opportunity once it has made a start. . . ." The accompanying *New Republic* editorial endorsed Kallen's thesis and added that "alien critics should beware of outlawing a political experiment which aroused in a whole nation an increased moral energy and dignified its activities by subordinating them to a deeply felt common purpose." *New Republic* 49 (January 12, 1927), pp. 207–13. Cited in John Patrick Diggins, "Mussolini's Italy: The View from America," Ph.D. diss., University of Southern California, 1964, pp. 214–17.

[55] Born in Ireland, David Croly became a distinguished journalist in New York City and rose to the editorship of the *New York World*. Croly organized the first Positivist Circle in the United States and financed an American speaking tour for the Comtian Henry Edgar. The Positivist Circle met at Croly's home, and in 1871 David Croly published *A Positivist Primer*. When Herbert was born in 1869, he was consecrated by his father to the Goddess Humanity, the symbol of Comte's Religion of Humanity. See the illuminating recent biography of Herbert by David W. Levy, *Herbert Croly of the New Republic* (Princeton, N.J.: Princeton University Press; 1985).

And what of Professor Dewey, the doyen of the pacifist intellectuals—turned drumbeaters for war? In a little known period of his life, John Dewey spent the immediate postwar years, 1919–21, teaching at Peking University and traveling in the Far East. China was then in a period of turmoil over the clauses of the Versailles Treaty that transferred the rights of dominance in Shantung from Germany to Japan. Japan had been promised this reward by the British and French in secret treaties in return for entering the war against Germany.

The Wilson Administration was torn between the two camps. On the one hand were those who wished to stand by the Allies' decision and who envisioned using Japan as a club against Bolshevik Russia in Asia. On the other were those who had already begun to sound the alarm about a Japanese menace and who were committed to China, often because of connections with the American Protestant missionaries who wished to defend and expand their extraterritorial powers of governance in China. The Wilson Administration, which had originally taken a pro-Chinese stand, reversed itself in the spring of 1919 and endorsed the Versailles provisions.

Into this complex situation John Dewey plunged, seeing no complexity and of course considering it unthinkable for either him or the United States to stay out of the entire fray. Dewey leaped into total support of the Chinese nationalist position, hailing the aggressive Young China movement and even endorsing the pro-missionary YMCA in China as "social workers." Dewey thundered that while "I didn't expect to be a jingo," that Japan must be called to account and that Japan is the great menace in Asia. Thus, scarcely had Dewey ceased being a champion of one terrible world war than he began to pave the way for an even greater one.[56]

[56] See Jerry Israel, *Progressivism and the Open Door: America and China, 1905–1921* (Pittsburgh: University of Pittsburgh Press, 1971).

ECONOMICS IN SERVICE OF THE STATE: THE EMPIRICISM OF RICHARD T. ELY

World War I was the apotheosis of the growing notion of intellectuals as servants of the State and junior partners in State rule. In the new fusion of intellectuals and State, each was of powerful aid to the other. Intellectuals could serve the State by apologizing for and supplying rationales for its deeds. Intellectuals were also needed to staff important positions as planners and controllers of the society and economy. The State could also serve intellectuals by restricting entry into, and thereby raising the income and the prestige of, the various occupations and professions. During World War I, historians were of particular importance in supplying the government with war propaganda, convincing the public of the unique evil of Germans throughout history and of the satanic designs of the Kaiser. Economists, particularly empirical economists and statisticians, were of great importance in the planning and control of the nation's wartime economy. Historians playing preeminent roles in the war propaganda machine have been studied fairly extensively; economists and statisticians, playing a less blatant and allegedly "value-free" role, have received far less attention.[57]

Although it is an outworn generalization to say that nineteenth century economists were stalwart champions of laissez faire, it is still true that deductive economic theory proved to be

---

[57] For a refreshingly acidulous portrayal of the actions of the historians in World War I, see C. Hartley Grattan, "The Historians Cut Loose," *American Mercury*, August 1927, reprinted in Haw Elmer Barnes, *In Quest of Truth and Justice*, 2nd ed. (Colorado Springs, Colo.: Ralph Myles Publisher, 1972), pp. 142–64. A more extended account is George T. Blakey, *Historians on the Homefront: American Propagandists for the Great War* (Lexington: University Press of Kentucky, 1970). Gruber, *Mars and Minerva*, deals with academia and social scientism, but concentrates an historians. James R. Mock and Cedric Larson, *Words that Won the War* (Princeton, N.J.: Princeton University Press, 1939), presents the story of the "Creel Committee," the Committee on Public Information, the official propaganda ministry during the war.

a mighty bulwark against government intervention. For, basically, economic theory showed the harmony and order inherent in the free market, as well as the counterproductive distortions and economic shackles imposed by state intervention. In order for statism to dominate the economics profession, then, it was important to discredit deductive theory. One of the most important ways of doing so was to advance the notion that, to be "genuinely scientific," economics had to eschew generalization and deductive laws and simply engage in empirical inquiry into the facts of history and historical institutions, hoping that somehow laws would eventually arise from these detailed investigations.

Thus the German Historical School, which managed to seize control of the economics discipline in Germany, fiercely proclaimed not only its devotion to statism and government control, but also its opposition to the "abstract" deductive laws of political economy. This was the first major group within the economics profession to champion what Ludwig von Mises was later to call "anti-economics." Gustav Schmoller, the leader of the Historical School, proudly declared that his and his colleagues' major task at the University of Berlin was to form "the intellectual bodyguard of the House of Hohenzollern."

During the 1880s and 1890s bright young graduate students in history and the social sciences went to Germany, the home of the Ph.D. degree, to obtain their doctorates. Almost to a man, they returned to the United States to teach in colleges and in the newly created graduate schools, imbued with the excitement of the "new" economics and political science. It was a "new" social science that lauded the German and Bismarckian development of a powerful welfare-warfare State, a State seemingly above all social classes, that fused the nation into an integrated and allegedly harmonious whole. The new society and polity was to be run by a powerful central government, cartelizing, dictating, arbitrating, and controlling, thereby eliminating competitive laissez-faire capitalism on the one hand and the threat of proletarian socialism on the other. And at or near the head of the new dispensation was to be the new breed of intellectuals, technocrats, and planners, directing, staffing, propagandizing, and "selflessly" promoting the common good while ruling and lording over the rest of society. In short, doing well by doing good. To the new breed of progressive and statist intellectuals in America, this was a heady vision indeed.

Richard T. Ely, virtually the founder of this new breed, was the leading progressive economist and also the teacher of most of the others. As an ardent postmillennialist pietist, Ely was convinced that he was serving God and Christ as well. Like so many pietists, Ely was born (in 1854) of solid Yankee and old Puritan stock, again in the midst of the fanatical Burned-Over District of western New York. Ely's father, Ezra, was an extreme Sabbatarian, preventing his family from playing games or reading books on Sunday, and so ardent a prohibitionist that, even though an impoverished, marginal farmer, he refused to grow barley, a crop uniquely suitable to his soil, because it would have been used to make that monstrously sinful product, beer.[58] Having been graduated from Columbia College in 1876, Ely went to Germany and received his Ph.D. from Heidelberg in 1879. In several decades of teaching at Johns Hopkins and then at Wisconsin, the energetic and empire-building Ely became enormously influential in American thought and politics. At Johns Hopkins he turned out a gallery of influential students and statist disciples in all fields of the social sciences as well as economics. These disciples were headed by the pro-union institutionalist economist John R. Commons, and included the social-control sociologists Edward Alsworth Ross and Albion W. Small; John H. Finlay, President of City College of New York; Dr. Albert Shaw, editor of the Review of Reviews and influential adviser and theoretician to Theodore

[58] See the useful biography of Ely, Benjamin G. Rader, *The Academic Mind and Reform: The Influence of Richard T. Ely in American Life* (Lexington: University Press of Kentucky, 1966).

Roosevelt; the municipal reformer Frederick C. Howe; and the historians Frederick Jackson Turner and J. Franklin Jameson. Newton D. Baker was trained by Ely at Hopkins, and Woodrow Wilson was also his student there, although there is no direct evidence of intellectual influence.

In the mid-1880s Richard Ely founded the American Economic Association in a conscious attempt to commit the economics profession to statism as against the older laissez-faire economists grouped in the Political Economy Club. Ely continued as secretary-treasurer of the AEA for seven years, until his reformer allies decided to weaken the association's commitment to statism in order to induce the laissez-faire economists to join the organization. At that point, Ely, in high dudgeon, left the AEA.

At Wisconsin in 1892, Ely formed a new School of Economics, Political Science, and History, surrounded himself with former students, and gave birth to the Wisconsin Idea which, with the help of John Commons, succeeded in passing a host of progressive measures for government regulation in Wisconsin. Ely and the others formed an unofficial but powerful brain trust for the progressive regime of Wisconsin Governor Robert M. La Follette, who got his start in Wisconsin politics as an advocate of prohibition. Though never a classroom student of Ely's, La Follette always referred to Ely as his teacher and as the molder of the Wisconsin Idea. And Theodore Roosevelt once declared that Ely "first introduced me to radicalism in economics and then made me sane in my radicalism."[59]

Ely was also one of the most prominent postmillennialist intellectuals of the era. He fervently believed that the State is God's chosen instrument for reforming and Christianizing the social order so that eventually Jesus would arrive and put an end to history. The State, declared Ely, "is religious in its

---

[59] Sidney Fine, *Laissez Faire and the General-Welfare State: A Study of Conflict in American Thought 1865–1901* (Ann Arbor: University of Michigan Press, 1956), pp. 239–40.

essence," and, furthermore, "God works through the State in carrying out His purposes more universally than through any other institution." The task of the church is to guide the State and utilize it in these needed reforms.[60]

An inveterate activist and organizer, Ely was prominent in the evangelical Chautauqua movement, and he founded there the "Christian Sociology" summer school, which infused the influential Chautauqua operation with the concepts and the personnel of the Social Gospel movement. Ely was a friend and close associate of Social Gospel leaders Revs. Washington Gladden, Walter Rauschenbusch, and Josiah Strong. With Strong and Commons, Ely organized the Institute of Christian Sociology.[61] Ely also founded and became the secretary of the Christian Social Union of the Episcopal Church, along with Christian Socialist W.D.P. Bliss. All of these activities were infused with postmillennial statism. Thus, the Institute of Christian Sociology was pledged to present God's "kingdom as the complete ideal of human society to be realized on earth." Moreover,

> Ely viewed the state as the greatest redemptive force in society. In Ely's eyes, government was the God-given

---

[60] Fine, *Laissez Faire*, pp. 180–181.

[61] John Rogers Commons was of old Yankee stock, descendant of John Rogers, Puritan martyr in England, and born in the Yankee area of the Western Reserve in Ohio and reared in Indiana. His Vermont mother was a graduate of the hotbed of pietism, Oberlin College, and she sent John to Oberlin in the hopes that he would become a minister. While in college, Commons and his mother launched a prohibitionist publication at the request of the Anti-Saloon League. After graduation, Commons went to Johns Hopkins to study under Ely, but flunked out of graduate school. See John R. Commons, *Myself* (Madison: University of Wisconsin Press, 1964). Also see Joseph Dorfman, *The Economic Mind in American Civilization* (New York: Viking, 1949), vol. 3, pp. 276–77; Mary O. Furner, *Advocacy and Objectivity: A Crisis in the Professionalization of American Social Science, 1865–1905* (Lexington: University Press of Kentucky, 1975), pp. 198–204.

> instrument through which we had to work. Its preeminence as a divine instrument was based on the post-Reformation abolition of the division between the sacred and the secular and on the State's power to implement ethical solutions to public problems. The same identification of sacred and secular which took place among liberal clergy enabled Ely to both divinize the state and socialize Christianity: he thought of government as God's main instrument of redemption. . . .[62]

When war came, Richard Ely was for some reason (perhaps because he was in his sixties) left out of the excitement of war work and economic planning in Washington. He bitterly regretted that "I have not had a more active part than I have had in this greatest war in the world's history."[63] But Ely made up for his lack as best he could; virtually from the start of the European war, he whooped it up for militarism, war, the "discipline" of conscription, and the suppression of dissent and "disloyalty" at home. A lifelong militarist, Ely had tried to volunteer for war service in the Spanish-American War, had called for the suppression of the Philippine insurrection, and was particularly eager for conscription and for forced labor for "loafers" during World War I. By 1915 Ely was agitating for immediate compulsory military service, and the following year he joined the ardently pro-war and heavily big business–influenced National Security League, where he called for the liberation of the German people from "autocracy."[64] In advocating con-

[62] Quandt, "Religion and Social Thought," pp. 402–03. Ely did not expect the millennial Kingdom to be far off. He believed that it was the task of the universities and of the social sciences "to teach the complexities of the Christian duty of brotherhood in order to arrive at the New Jerusalem "which we are all eagerly awaiting." The church's mission was to attack every evil institution, "until the earth becomes a new earth, and all its cities, cities of God."

[63] Gruber, *Mars and Minerva*, p. 114.

[64] See Rader, *Academic Mind*, pp. 181–91. On top big business affiliations of National Security League leaders, especially J.P. Morgan and others in the

scription, Ely was neatly able to combine moral, economic, and prohibitionist arguments for the draft: "The moral effect of taking boys off street corners and out of saloons and drilling them is excellent, and the economic effects are likewise beneficial."[65] Indeed, conscription for Ely served almost as a panacea for all ills. So enthusiastic was he about the World War I experience that Ely again prescribed his favorite cure-all to alleviate the 1929 depression. He proposed a permanent peacetime "industrial army" engaged in public works and manned by conscripting youth for strenuous physical labor. This conscription would instill into America's youth the essential "military ideals of hardihood and discipline," a discipline once provided by life on the farm but unavailable to the bulk of the populace now growing up in the effete cities. This small, standing conscript army could then speedily absorb the unemployed during depressions. Under the command of "an economic general staff," the industrial army would "go to work to relieve distress with all the vigor and resources of brain and brawn that we employed in the World War."[66]

Morgan ambit, see C. Hartley Grattan, *Why We Fought* (New York Vanguard Press, 1929) pp. 117–18, and Robert D. Ward, "The Origin and Activities of the National Security League, 1914–1919," *Mississippi Valley Historical Review* 47 (June 1960): 51–65.

[65] The Chamber of Commerce of the United States spelled out the long-run economic benefit of conscription, that for America's youth it would "substitute a period of helpful discipline for a period of demoralizing freedom from restraint." John Patrick Finnegan, *Against the Specter of Dragon: The Campaign for American Military Preparedness, 1914–1917* (Westport, Conn.: Greenwood Press, 1974), p. 110. On the broad and enthusiastic support given to the draft by the Chamber of Commerce, see Chase C. Mooney and Martha E. Layman, "Some Phases of the Compulsory Military Training Movement, 1914–1920," *Mississippi Historical Review* 38 (March 1952): 640.

[66] Richard T. Ely, *Hard Times: The Way in and the Way Out* (1931), cited in Joseph Dorfman, *The Economic Mind in American Civilization* (New York: Viking, 1949). vol. 5, p. 671; and in Leuchtenburg, "The New Deal," p. 94.

Deprived of a position in Washington, Ely made the stamping out of "disloyalty" at home his major contribution to the war effort. He called for the total suspension of academic freedom for the duration. Any professor, he declared, who stated "opinions which hinder us in this awful struggle" should be "fired" if not indeed "shot." The particular focus of Ely's formidable energy was a zealous campaign to try to get his old ally in Wisconsin politics, Robert M. La Follette, expelled from the US Senate for continuing to oppose America's participation in the war. Ely declared that his "blood boils" at La Follette's "treason" and attacks on war profiteering. Throwing himself into the battle, Ely founded and became president of the Madison chapter of the Wisconsin Loyalty Legion and mounted a campaign to expel La Follette.[67] The campaign was meant to mobilize the Wisconsin faculty and to support the ultrapatriotic and ultrahawkish activities of Theodore Roosevelt. Ely wrote to TR that "we must crush La Follettism." In his unremitting campaign against the Wisconsin Senator, Ely thundered that La Follette "has been of more help to the Kaiser than a quarter of a million troops."[68] "Empiricism" rampant.

The faculty of the University of Wisconsin was stung by charges throughout the state and the country that its failure to denounce La Follette was proof that the university—long affiliated with La Follette in state politics—supported his disloyal antiwar policies. Prodded by Ely, Commons, and others, the university's War Committee drew up and circulated a petition, signed by the university president, all the deans, and over 90 percent of the faculty, that provided one of the more striking

[67] Ely drew up a super-patriotic pledge for the Madison chapter of the Loyalty Legion, pledging its members to "stamp out disloyalty." The pledge also expressed unqualified support for the Espionage Act and vowed to "work against La Follettism in all its anti-war forms." Rader, *Academic Mind*, pp. 183ff.

[68] Gruber, *Mars and Minerva*, p. 207.

examples in United States history of academic truckling to the State apparatus. None too subtly using the constitutional verbiage for treason, the petition protested "against those utterances and actions of Senator La Follette which have given aid and comfort to Germany and her allies in the present war; we deplore his failure loyally to support the government in the prosecution of the war."[69]

Behind the scenes, Ely tried his best to mobilize America's historians against La Follette, to demonstrate that he had given aid and comfort to the enemy. Ely was able to enlist the services of the National Board of Historical Service, the propaganda agency established by professional historians for the duration of the war, and of the government's own propaganda arm, the Committee on Public Information. Warning that the effort must remain secret, Ely mobilized historians under the aegis of these organizations to research German and Austrian newspapers and journals to try to build a record of La Follette's alleged influence, "indicating the encouragement he has given Germany." The historian E. Merton Coulter revealed the objective spirit animating these researches: "I understand it is to be an unbiased and candid account of the Senator's [La Follette's] course and its effect—but we all know it can lead but to one conclusion—something little short of treason."[70]

Professor Gruber well notes that this campaign to get La Follette was "a remarkable example of the uses of scholarship for espionage. It was a far cry from the disinterested search for truth for a group of professors to mobilize a secret research campaign to find ammunition to destroy the political career of a United States senator who did not share their view of the war."[71] In any event, no evidence was turned up, the movement

---

[69] Ibid., p. 207.

[70] Ibid., pp. 208, 208n.

[71] Ibid., pp. 209–10. In his autobiography, written in 1938, Richard Ely rewrote history to cover up his ignominious role in the get–La Follette campaign. He

failed, and the Wisconsin professoriat began to move away in distrust from the Loyalty Legion.[72]

After the menace of the Kaiser had been extirpated, the Armistice found Professor Ely, along with his compatriots in the National Security League, ready to segue into the next round of patriotic repression. During Ely's anti–La Follette research campaign he had urged investigation of "the kind of influence which he [La Follette] has exerted against our country in Russia." Ely pointed out that modem "democracy" requires a "high degree of conformity" and that therefore the "most serious menace" of Bolshevism, which Ely depicted as "social disease germs," must be fought "with repressive measures."

By 1924, however, Richard T. Ely's career of repression was over, and what is more, in a rare instance of the workings of poetic justice, he was hoisted with his own petard. In 1922 the much-traduced Robert La Follette was reelected to the Senate and also swept the Progressives back into power in the state of Wisconsin. By 1924 the Progressives had gained control of the Board of Regents, and they moved to cut off the water of their former academic ally and empire-builder. Ely then felt it prudent to move out of Wisconsin together with his Institute, and while he lingered for some years at Northwestern, the heyday of Ely's fame and fortune was over.

---

acknowledged signing the faculty petition, but then had the temerity to claim that he "was not one of the ring-leaders, as La Follette thought, in circulating this petition. . . ." There is no mention of his secret research campaign against La Follette.

[72] For more an the anti–La Follette campaign, see H.C. Peterson and Gilbert C. Fite, *Opponents of War: 1917–1918* (Madison: University of Wisconsin Press, 1957), pp. 68–72; Paul L. Murphy, World War I and the Origin of Civil Liberties in the United States (New York: W.W. Norton, 1979), p. 120; and Belle Case La Follette and Fola La Follette, *Robert M. LaFollette* (New York: Macmillan, 1953), vol. 2.

ECONOMICS IN SERVICE OF THE STATE: GOVERNMENT AND STATISTICS

Statistics is a vital, though much underplayed, requisite of modern government. Government could not even presume to control, regulate, or plan any portion of the economy without the service of its statistical bureaus and agencies. Deprive government of its statistics and it would be a blind and helpless giant, with no idea whatever of what to do or where to do it.

It might be replied that business firms, too, need statistics in order to function. But business needs for statistics are far less in quantity and also different in quality. Business may need statistics in its own micro area of the economy, but only on its prices and costs; it has little need for broad collections of data or for sweeping, holistic aggregates. Business could perhaps rely on its own privately collected and unshared data. Furthermore, much entrepreneurial knowledge is qualitative, not enshrined in quantitative data, and of a particular time, area, and location. But government bureaucracy could do nothing if forced to be confined to qualitative data. Deprived of profit and loss tests for efficiency, or of the need to serve consumers efficiently, conscripting both capital and operating costs from taxpayers, and forced to abide by fixed, bureaucratic rules, modern government shorn of masses of statistics could do virtually nothing.[73]

Hence the enormous importance of World War I, not only in providing the power and the precedent for a collectivized economy, but also in greatly accelerating the advent of statisticians and statistical agencies of government, many of which

---

[73] Thus, T.W. Hutchison, from a very different perspective, notes the contrast between Carl Menger's stress on the beneficent, unplanned phenomena of society, such as the free market, and the growth of "social self-consciousness" and government planning. Hutchison recognizes that a crucial component of that social self-consciousness is government statistics. T.W. Hutchison, *A Review of Economic Doctrines, 1870–1929* (Oxford: Clarendon Press, 1953), pp. 150–51, 427.

(and who) remained in government, ready for the next leap forward of power.

Richard T. Ely, of course, championed the new empirical "look and see" approach, with the aim of fact-gathering to "mold the forces at work in society and to improve existing conditions."[74] More importantly, one of the leading authorities on the growth of government expenditure has linked it with statistics and empirical data: "Advance in economic science and statistics strengthened belief in the possibilities of dealing with social problems by collective action. It made for increase in the statistical and other fact-finding activities of government."[75] As early as 1863, Samuel B. Ruggles, American delegate to the International Statistical Congress in Berlin, proclaimed that "statistics are the very eyes of the statesman, enabling him to survey and scan with clear and comprehensive vision the whole structure and economy of the body politic."[76]

---

[74] Fine, *Laissez-Faire*, p. 207.

[75] Solomon Fabricant, *The Trend of Government Activity in the United States since 1900* (New York: National Bureau of Economic Research, 1952), p. 143. Similarly, an authoritative work on the growth of government in England puts it this way: "The accumulation of factual information about social conditions and the development of economics and the social sciences increased the pressure for government intervention. . . . As statistics improved and students of social conditions multiplied, the continued existence of such conditions was kept before the public. Increasing knowledge of them aroused influential circles and furnished working class movements with factual weapons." Moses Abramovitz and Vera F. Eliasberg, *The Growth of Public Employment in Great Britain* (Princeton: National Bureau of Economic Research, 1957), pp. 22–23, 30. Also see M.I. Cullen, *The Statistical Movement in Early Victorian Britain: The Foundations of Empirical Social Research* (New York: Barnes & Noble, 1975).

[76] See Joseph Dorfman, "The Role of the German Historical School in American Economic Thought." *American Economic Review, Papers and Proceedings* 45 (May 1955), p. 18. George Hildebrand remarked on the inductive emphasis of the German Historical School that "perhaps there is, then, some connection between this kind of teaching and the popularity of

Conversely, this means that stripped of these means of vision, the statesman would no longer be able to meddle, control and plan.

Moreover, government statistics are clearly needed for specific types of intervention. Government could not intervene to alleviate unemployment unless statistics of unemployment were collected—and so the impetus for such collection. Carroll D. Wright, one of the first Commissioners of Labor in the United States, was greatly influenced by the famous statistician and German Historical School member, Ernst Engel, head of the Royal Statistical Bureau of Prussia. Wright sought the collection of unemployment statistics for that reason, and in general, for "the amelioration of unfortunate industrial and social relations." Henry Carter Adams, a former student of Engel's, and, like Ely, a statist and progressive "new economist," established the Statistical Bureau of the Interstate Commerce Commission, believing that "ever increasing statistical activity by the government was essential—for the sake of controlling naturally monopolistic industries." And Professor Irving Fisher of Yale, eager for government to stabilize the price level, conceded that he wrote *The Making of Index Numbers* to solve the problem of the unreliability of index numbers. "Until this difficulty could be met, stabilization could scarcely be expected to become a reality."

Carroll Wright was a Bostonian and a progressive reformer. Henry Carter Adams, the son of a New England pietist Congregationalist preacher on missionary duty in Iowa, studied for the ministry at his father's alma mater, Andover Theological Seminary, but soon abandoned this path. Adams devised the accounting system of the Statistical Bureau of the ICC. This

---

crude ideas of physical planning in more recent times." George H. Hildebrand, "International Flow of Economic Ideas-Discussion," ibid., p. 37.

system "served as a model for the regulation of public utilities here and throughout the world."[77]

Irving Fisher was the son of a Rhode Island Congregationalist pietist preacher, and his parents were both of old Yankee stock, his mother a strict Sabbatarian. As befitted what his son and biographer called his "crusading spirit," Fisher was an inveterate reformer, urging the imposition of numerous progressive measures including Esperanto, simplified spelling, and calendar reform. He was particularly enthusiastic about purging the world of "such iniquities of civilization as alcohol, tea, coffee, tobacco, refined sugar, and bleached white flour."[78]

During the 1920s Fisher was the leading prophet of that so-called New Era in economics and in society. He wrote three books during the 1920s praising the noble experiment of prohibition, and he lauded Governor Benjamin Strong and the Federal Reserve System for following his advice and expanding money and credit so as to keep the wholesale price level virtually constant. Because of the Fed's success in imposing Fisherine price stabilization, Fisher was so sure that there could be no depression that as late as 1930 he wrote a book claiming that there was and could be no stock crash and that stock prices would quickly rebound. Throughout the 1920s Fisher insisted that since wholesale prices remained constant, there was nothing amiss about the wild boom in stocks. Meanwhile he put his theories into practice by heavily investing his heiress wife's considerable fortune in the stock market. After the crash he

[77] Dorfman, "Role," p. 23. On Wright and Adams, see Joseph Dorfman, *The Economic Mind in American Civilization* (New York: Viking Press, 1949), vol. 3, 164–74, 123; and Boyer, *Urban Masses*, p. 163. Furthermore, the first professor of statistics in the United States, Roland P. Falkner, was a devoted student of Engel's and a translator of the works of Engel's assistant, August Meitzen.

[78] Irving Norton Fisher, *My Father Irving Fisher* (New York: Comet Press, 1956), pp. 146–47. Also for Fisher, see *Irving Fisher, Stabilised Money* (London: Allen & Unwin, 1935), p. 383.

frittered away his sister-in-law's money when his wife's fortune was depleted, at the same time calling frantically on the federal government to inflate money and credit and to re-inflate stock prices to their 1929 levels. Despite his dissipation of two family fortunes, Fisher managed to blame almost everyone except himself for the debacle.[79]

As we shall see, in view of the importance of Wesley Clair Mitchell in the burgeoning of government statistics in World War I, Mitchell's view on statistics are of particular importance.[80] Mitchell, an institutionalist and student of Thorstein Veblen, was one of the prime founders of modern statistical inquiry in economics and clearly aspired to lay the basis for "scientific" government planning. As Professor Dorfman, friend and student of Mitchell's, put it:

> "clearly the type of social invention most needed today is one that offers definite techniques through which the social system can be controlled and operated to the optimum advantage of its members." (Quote from Mitchell.) To this end he constantly sought to extend, improve and refine the gathering and compilation of data. . . . Mitchell believed that business-cycle analysis . . . might

---

[79] Fisher, *My Father*, pp. 264–67. On Fisher's role and influence during this period, see Murray N. Rothbard, *America's Great Depression*, 4th ed. (New York: Richardson & Snyder, 1983). Also see Joseph S. Davis, *The World Between the Wars, 1919–39, An Economist's View* (Baltimore: Johns Hopkins University Press, 1975), p. 194; and Melchior Palyi, *The Twilight of Gold, 1914–1936: Myth and Realities* (Chicago: Henry Regnery, 1972), pp. 240, 249.

[80] Wesley C. Mitchell was of old Yankee pietist stock. His grandparents were farmers in Maine and then in Western New York. His father followed the path of many Yankees in migrating to a farm in northern Illinois. Mitchell attended the University of Chicago, where he was strongly influenced by Veblen and John Dewey. Dorfman, *Economic Mind*, vol. 3, p. 456.

> indicate the means to the achievement of orderly social control of business activity.[81]

Or, as Mitchell's wife and collaborator stated in her memoirs:

> he [Mitchell] envisioned the great contribution that government could make to the understanding of economic and social problems if the statistical data gathered independently by various Federal agencies were systematized and planned so that the interrelationships among them could be studied. The idea of developing social statistics, *not merely as a record but as a basis for planning*, emerged early in his own work.[82]

Particularly important in the expansion of statistics in World War I was the growing insistence, by progressive intellectuals and corporate liberal businessmen alike, that democratic decision-making must be increasingly replaced by the administrative and technocratic. Democratic or legislative decisions were messy, "inefficient," and might lead to a significant curbing of statism, as had happened in the heyday of the Democratic party during the nineteenth century. But if decisions were largely administrative and technocratic, the burgeoning of state power could continue unchecked. The collapse of the laissez-faire creed of the Democrats in 1896 left a power vacuum in government that administrative and corporatist types were eager to fill.

Increasingly, then, such powerful corporatist big business groups as the National Civic Federation disseminated the idea that governmental decisions should be in the hands of the efficient technician, the allegedly value-free expert. In short, government, in virtually all of its aspects, should be "taken out of politics." And statistical research with its aura of empiricism,

---

[81] Dorfman, *Economic Mind*, vol. 4, pp. 376, 361.

[82] Emphasis added. Lucy Sprague Mitchell, *Two Lives* (New York: Simon and Schuster, 1953), p. 363. For more on this entire topic, see Murray N. Rothbard, "The Politics of Political Economists: Comment," *Quarterly Journal of Economics* 74 (November 1960): 659–65.

quantitative precision, and nonpolitical value-freedom, was in the forefront of such emphasis. In the municipalities, an increasingly powerful progressive reform movement shifted decisions from elections in neighborhood wards to citywide professional managers and school superintendents. As a corollary, political power was increasingly shifted from working class and ethnic German Lutheran and Catholic wards to upper-class pietist business groups.[83]

By the time World War I arrived in Europe, a coalition of progressive intellectuals and corporatist businessmen was ready to go national in sponsoring allegedly objective statistical research institutes and think tanks. Their views have been aptly summed up by David Eakins:

> The conclusion being drawn by these people by 1915 was that fact-finding and policymaking had to be isolated from class struggle and freed from political pressure groups. The reforms that would lead to industrial peace and social order, these experts were coming to believe, could only be derived from data determined by objective fact-finders (such as themselves) and under the auspices of sober and respectable organizations (such as only they could construct). The capitalist system could be improved only by a single-minded reliance upon experts detached from the hurly-burly of democratic policy-making. The emphasis was upon efficiency—and democratic policymaking was inefficient. An approach to the making of national economic and social policy outside traditional democratic political processes was

---

[83] See in particular James Weinstein, *The Corporate Ideal in the Liberal State, 1900–1918* (Boston: Beacon Press, 1968); and Samuel P. Hays, "The Politics of Reform in Municipal Government in the Progressive Era," *Pacific Northwest Quarterly* 59 (October 1961), pp. 157–69.

> thus emerging before the United States formally entered World War I.[84]

Several corporatist businessmen and intellectuals moved at about the same time toward founding such statistical research institutes. In 1906–07, Jerome D. Greene, secretary of the Harvard University Corporation, helped found an elite Tuesday Evening Club at Harvard to explore important issues in economics and the social sciences. In 1910 Greene rose to an even more powerful post as general manager of the new Rockefeller Institute for Medical Research, and three years later Greene became secretary and CEO of the powerful philanthropic organization, the Rockefeller Foundation. Greene immediately began to move toward establishing a Rockefeller-funded institute for economic research, and in March 1914 he called an exploratory group together in New York, chaired by his friend and mentor in economics, the first Dean of the Harvard Graduate School of Business, Edwin F. Gay. The developing idea was that Gay would become head of a new, "scientific" and "impartial" organization, The Institute of Economic Research, which would gather statistical facts, and that Wesley Mitchell would be its director.[85]

---

[84] David Eakins, "The Origins of Corporate Liberal Policy Research, 1916–1922: The Political-Economic Expert and the Decline of Public Debate," in Israel, ed., *Building the Organizational Society*, p. 161.

[85] Herbert Heaton, *Edwin F. Gay, A Scholar in Action* (Cambridge, Mass.: Harvard University Press, 1952). Edwin Gay was born in Detroit of old New England stock. His father had been born in Boston and went into his father-in-law's lumber business in Michigan. Gay's mother was the daughter of a wealthy preacher and lumberman. Gay entered the University of Michigan, was heavily influenced by the teaching of John Dewey, and then stayed in graduate school in Germany for over a dozen years, finally obtaining his Ph.D. in economic history at the University of Berlin. The major German influences on Gay were Gustav Schmoller, head of the Historical School, who emphasized that economics must be an "inductive science," and Adolf Wagner, also at the University of Berlin, who favored large-scale government intervention in the economy in behalf of Christian ethics. Back at Harvard, Gay was the

However, opposing advisers to John D. Rockefeller, Jr., won out over Greene, and the institute plan was scuttled.[86] Mitchell and Gay pressed on, with the lead now taken by Mitchell's longtime friend, chief statistician and vice president of AT&T, Malcolm C. Rorty. Rorty lined up support for the idea from a number of progressive statisticians and businessmen, including Chicago publisher of business books and magazines, Arch W. Shaw; E.H. Goodwin of the US Chamber of Commerce; Magnus Alexander, statistician and assistant to the president of General Electric, like AT&T, a Morgan-oriented concern; John R. Commons, economist and aide-de-camp to Richard T. Ely at Wisconsin; and Nahum I. Stone, statistician, former Marxist, a leader in the "scientific management" movement, and labor manager for the Hickey Freeman clothing company. This group was in the process of forming a "Committee on National Income" when the United States entered the war, and they were forced to shelve their plans temporarily.[87] After the

major single force, in collaboration with the Boston Chamber of Commerce, in pushing through a factory inspection act in Massachusetts, and in early 1911 Gay became president of the Massachusetts branch of the American Association for Labor Legislation, an organization founded by Richard T. Ely and dedicated to agitating for government intervention in the area of labor unions, minimum wage rates, unemployment, public works, and welfare.

[86] On the pulling and hauling among Rockefeller advisers on The Institute of Economic Research, see David M. Grossman, "American Foundations and the Support of Economic Research, 1913–29," *Minerva* 22 (Spring–Summer, 1982): 62–72.

[87] See Eakins, "Origins," pp. 166–67; Grossman, "American Foundations," pp. 76–78; Heaton, Edwin F. Gay. On Stone, see Dorfman, *Economic Mind*, vol. 4, pp. 42, 60–61; and Samuel Haber, *Efficiency and Uplift: Scientific Management in the Progressive Era 1890–1920* (Chicago: University of Chicago Press, 1964), pp. 152, 165. During his Marxist period, Stone had translated Marx's *Poverty of Philosophy*.

war, however, the group set up the National Bureau of Economic Research, in 1920.[88]

While the National Bureau was not to take final shape until after the war, another organization, created on similar lines, successfully won Greene's and Rockefeller's support. In 1916 they were persuaded by Raymond B. Fosdick to found the Institute for Government Research (IGR).[89] The IGR was slightly different in focus from the National Bureau group, as it grew directly out of municipal progressive reform and the political science profession. One of the important devices used by the municipal reformers was the private bureau of municipal research, which tried to seize decision-making from allegedly "corrupt" democratic bodies on behalf of efficient, nonpartisan organizations headed by progressive technocrats and social scientists. In 1910 President William Howard Taft, intrigued with the potential for centralizing power in a chief executive inherent in the idea of the executive budget, appointed the "father of the budget idea," the political scientist Frederick D. Cleveland, as head of a Commission on Economy and Efficiency. Cleveland was the director of the New York Bureau of Municipal Research. The Cleveland Commission also included political scientist and municipal reformer Frank Goodnow, professor of public law at Columbia University, first president of the American Political Science Association and president of Johns Hopkins; and William Franklin Willoughby, former student of Ely, Assistant Director of the Bureau of Census, and later President of the American Association for Labor Legislation.[90] The Cleveland Commission was delighted to tell President

---

[88] See Guy Alchon, *The Invisible Hand of Planning: Capitalism, Social Science, and the State in the 1920's* (Princeton, N.J.: Princeton University Press, 1985), pp. 54ff.

[89] Collier and Horowitz, *The Rockefellers*, p. 140.

[90] Eakins, "Origins," p. 168. Also see Furner, *Advocacy and Objectivity*, pp. 282–86.

Taft precisely what he wanted to hear. The Commission recommended sweeping administrative changes that would provide a Bureau of Central Administrative Control to form a "consolidated information and statistical arm of the entire national government." And at the heart of the new Bureau would be the Budget Division, which was to develop, at the behest of the president, and then present "an annual program of business for the Federal Government to be financed by Congress."[91]

When Congress balked at the Cleveland Commission's recommendations, the disgruntled technocrats decided to establish an Institute for Government Research in Washington to battle for these and similar reforms. With funding secured from the Rockefeller Foundation, the IGR was chaired by Goodnow, with Willoughby as its director.[92] Then Robert S. Brookings assumed responsibility for the financing.

When America entered the war, present and future NBER and IGR leaders were all over Washington, key figures and statisticians in the collectivized war economy.

---

[91] Stephen Skowronek, *Building a New American State: The Expansion of the National Administrative Capacities, 1877–1920* (Cambridge: Cambridge University Press, 1982), pp. 187–88.

[92] Vice-chairman of the IGR was retired St. Louis merchant and lumberman and former president of Washington University of St. Louis, Robert S. Brookings. Secretary of the IGR was James F. Curtis, formerly Assistant Secretary of the Treasury under Taft and now secretary and deputy governor of the New York Federal Reserve Bank. Others on the board of the IGR were ex-President Taft; railroad executive Frederick A. Delano, uncle of Franklin D. Roosevelt and member of the Federal Reserve Board; Arthur T. Hadley, economist and president of Yale; Charles C. Van Hise, progressive president of the University of Wisconsin, and ally of Ely; reformer and influential young Harvard Law professor, Felix Frankfurter; Theodore N. Vail, chairman of AT&T; progressive engineer and businessman, Herbert C. Hoover; and financier R. Fulton Cutting, an officer of the New York Bureau of Municipal Research. Eakins, "Origins," pp. 168–69.

By far the most powerful of the growing number of economists and statisticians involved in World War I was Edwin F. Gay. Arch W. Shaw, an enthusiast for rigid wartime planning of economic resources, was made head of the new Commercial Economy Board by the Council for National Defense as soon as America entered the war.[93] Shaw, who had taught at and served on the administrative board of Harvard Business School, staffed the board with Harvard Business people; the secretary was Harvard economist Melvin T. Copeland, and other members included Dean Gay.

The board, which later became the powerful Conservation Division of the War Industries Board, focused on restricting competition in industry by eliminating the number and variety of products and by imposing compulsory uniformity, all in the name of "conservation" of resources to aid the war effort. For example, garment firms had complained loudly of severe competition because of the number and variety of styles, and so Gay urged the garment firms to form a trade association to work with the government in curbing the surfeit of competition. Gay also tried to organize the bakers so that they would not follow the usual custom of taking back stale and unsold bread from retail outlets. By the end of 1917, Gay was tired of using voluntary persuasion and was urging the government to use compulsory measures.

Gay's major power came in early 1918 when the Shipping Board, which had officially nationalized all ocean shipping, determined to restrict drastically the use of ships for civilian trade and to use the bulk of shipping for transport of American troops to France. Appointed in early January 1918 as merely a "special expert" by the Shipping Board, Gay in a brief time became the key figure in redirecting shipping from civilian to

---

[93] On the Commercial Economy Board, see Grosvenor B. Clarkson, *Industrial America in the World War: The Strategy Behind the Line, 1917–1918* (Boston: Houghton Mifilin, 1923), pp. 211ff.

military use. Soon Edwin Gay had become a member of the War Trade Board and head of its statistical department, which issued restrictive licenses for permitted imports; head of the statistical department of the Shipping Board; representative of the Shipping Board on the War Trade Board; head of the statistical committee of the Department of Labor; head of the Division of Planning and Statistics of the War Industries Board (WIB); and, above all, head of the new Central Bureau of Planning and Statistics. The Central Bureau was organized in the fall of 1918, when President Wilson asked WIB chairman Bernard Baruch to produce a monthly survey of all the government's war activities. This "conspectus" evolved into the Central Bureau, responsible directly to the president. The importance of the bureau is noted by a recent historian:

> The new Bureau represented the "peak" statistical division of the mobilization, becoming its "seer and prophet" for the duration, coordinating over a thousand employees engaged in research and, as the agency responsible for giving the president a concise picture of the entire economy, becoming the closest approximation to a "central statistical commission." During the latter stages of the war it set up a clearinghouse of statistical work, organized liaisons with the statistical staff of all the war boards, and centralized the data production process for the entire war bureaucracy. By the war's end, Wesley Mitchell recalled, "we were in a fair way to develop for the first time a systematic organization of federal statistics."[94]

Within a year, Edwin Gay had risen from a special expert to the unquestioned czar of a giant network of federal statistical agencies, with over a thousand researchers and statisticians working under his direct control. It is no wonder then that Gay,

---

[94] Alchon, *Invisible Hand*, p. 29. Mitchell headed the price statistics section of the Price-Fixing Committee of the War Industries Board.

instead of being enthusiastic about the American victory he had worked so hard to secure, saw the Armistice as "almost a personal blow" that plunged him "into the slough of despond." All of his empire of statistics and control had just been coming together and developing into a mighty machine when suddenly "came that wretched Armistice."[95] Truly a tragedy of peace.

Gay tried valiantly to keep the war machinery going, continually complaining because many of his aides were leaving and bitterly denouncing the "hungry pack" who, for some odd reason, were clamoring for an immediate end to all wartime controls, including those closest to his heart, foreign trade and shipping. But one by one, despite the best efforts of Baruch and many of the wartime planners, the WIB and other war agencies disappeared.[96] For a while, Gay pinned his hopes on his Central Bureau of Planning and Statistics (CBPS), which, in a fierce bout of bureaucratic infighting, he attempted to make the key economic and statistical group advising the American negotiators at the Versailles peace conference, thereby displacing the team of historians and social scientists assembled by Colonel House in the Inquiry. Despite an official victory, and an eight volume report of the CBPS delivered to Versailles by the head of CBPS European team, John Foster Dulles of the War Trade Board, the bureau had little influence over the final treaty.[97]

Peace having finally and irrevocably arrived, Edwin Gay, backed by Mitchell, tried his best to have the CBPS kept as a permanent, peacetime organization. Gay argued that the agency, with himself of course remaining as its head, could

---

[95] Heaton, *Edwin Gay*, p. 129.

[96] See Rothbard, "War Collectivism," pp. 100–12.

[97] See Heaton, *Edwin Gay*, pp. 129ff.; and the excellent book on the Inquiry, Lawrence E. Gelfand, *The Inquiry: American Preparations for Peace, 1917–1919* (New Haven, Conn.: Yale University Press, 1963), pp. 166–68, 177–78.

provide continuing data to the League of Nations, and above all could serve as the president's own eyes and ears and mold the sort of executive budget envisioned by the old Taft Commission. CBPS staff member and Harvard economist Edmund E. Day contributed a memorandum outlining specific tasks for the bureau to aid in demobilization and reconstruction, as well as rationale for the bureau becoming a permanent part of government. One thing it could do was to make a "continuing canvass" of business conditions in the United States. As Gay put it to President Wilson, using a favorite organicist analogy, a permanent board would serve "as a nervous system to the vast and complex organization of the government, furnishing to the controlling brain [the president] the information necessary for directing the efficient operation of the various members."[98] Although the President was "very cordial" to Gay's plan, Congress refused to agree, and on June 30, 1919 the Central Bureau of Planning and Statistics was finally terminated, along with the War Trade Board. Edwin Gay would now have to seek employment in, if not the private, at least the quasi-independent, sector.

But Gay and Mitchell were not to be denied. Nor would the Brookings-Willoughby group. Their objective would be met more gradually and by slightly different means. Gay became editor of the *New York Evening Post* under the aegis of its new owner and Gay's friend, J.P. Morgan partner Thomas W. Lamont. Gay also helped to form and become first president of the National Bureau of Economic Research in 1920, with Wesley C. Mitchell as research director. The Institute for Government Research achieved its major objective, establishing a Budget Bureau in the Treasury Department in 1921, with the director of the IGR, William F. Willoughby, helping to draft

---

[98] Heaton, *Edwin Gay*, p. 135. Also see Alchon, *Invisible Hand*, pp. 35–36.

the bill that established the bureau.[99] The IGR people soon expanded their role to include economics, establishing an Institute of Economics headed by Robert Brookings and Arthur T. Hadley of Yale, with economist Harold G. Moulton as director.[100] The institute, funded by the Carnegie Corporation, would be later merged, along with the IGR, into the Brookings Institution. Edwin Gay also moved into the foreign policy field by becoming secretary-treasurer and head of the Research Committee of the new and extremely influential organization, the Council on Foreign Relations (CFR).[101]

And finally, in the field of government statistics, Gay and Mitchell found a more gradual but longer-range route to power via collaboration with Herbert Hoover, soon to be Secretary of Commerce. No sooner had Hoover assumed the post in early 1921 when he expanded the Advisory Committee on the Census to include Gay, Mitchell, and other economists and then launched the monthly Survey of Current Business. The Survey was designed to supplement the informational activities of cooperating trade associations and, by supplying business information, aid these associations in Hoover's aim of cartelizing their respective industries.

---

[99] In 1939 the Bureau of the Budget would be transferred to the Executive Office, thus completing the IGR objective.

[100] Moulton was a professor of economics at the University of Chicago, and vice-president of the Chicago Association of Commerce. See Eakins, "Origins," pp. 172–77; Dorfman, *Economic Mind*, vol. 4, pp. 11, 195–97.

[101] Gay had been recommended to the group by one of its founders, Thomas W. Lamont. It was Gay's suggestion that the CFR begin its major project by establishing an "authoritative" journal, *Foreign Affairs*. And it was Gay who selected his Harvard historian colleague Archibald Cary Coolidge as the first editor and the *New York Post* reporter Hamilton Fish Armstrong as assistant editor and executive director of the CFR. See Lawrence H. Shoup and William Minter, *Imperial Brain Trust: The Council on Foreign Relations and United States Foreign Policy* (New York: Monthly Review Press, 1977), pp. 16–19, 105, 110.

Secrecy in business operations is a crucial weapon of competition, and conversely, publicity and sharing of information is an important tool of cartels in policing their members. The Survey of Current Business made available the current production, sales, and inventory data supplied by cooperating industries and technical journals. Hoover also hoped that by building on these services, eventually "the statistical program could provide the knowledge and foresight necessary to combat panic or speculative conditions, prevent the development of diseased industries, and guide decision-making so as to iron out rather than accentuate the business cycle."[102] In promoting his cartelization doctrine, Hoover met resistance both from some businessmen who resisted prying questionnaires and sharing competitive secrets and from the Justice Department. But, a formidable empire-builder, Herbert Hoover managed to grab statistical services from the Treasury Department and to establish a "waste elimination division" to organize businesses and trade associations to continue and expand the wartime "conservation" program of compulsory uniformity and restriction of the number and variety of competitive products. As assistant secretary to head up this program, Hoover secured engineer and publicist Frederick Feiker, an associate of Arch Shaw's business publication empire. Hoover also found a top assistant and lifelong disciple in Brigadier General Julius Klein, a protégé of Edwin Gay's, who had headed the Latin American division of the Bureau of Foreign and Domestic Commerce. As the new head of the bureau, Klein organized seventeen new export commodity divisions—reminiscent of commodity sections during wartime collectivism—each with "experts" drawn from the respective industries and each organizing regular cooperation

[102] Ellis W. Hawley, "Herbert Hoover and Economic Stabilization, 1921–22," in E. Hawley, ed., *Herbert Hoover as Secretary of Commerce: Studies in New Era Thought and Practice* (Iowa City: University of Iowa Press, 1981), p. 52.

with parallel industrial advisory committees. And through it all Herbert Hoover made a series of well-publicized speeches during 1921, spelling out how a well-designed government trade program, as well as a program in the domestic economy, could act both as a stimulant to recovery and as a permanent "stabilizer," while avoiding such unfortunate measures as abolishing tariffs or cutting wage rates. The best weapon, both in foreign and domestic trade, was to "eliminate waste" by a "cooperative mobilization" of government and industry.[103]

A month after the Armistice, the American Economic Association and the American Statistical Association met jointly in Richmond, Virginia. The presidential addresses were delivered by men in the forefront of the exciting new world of government planning, aided by social science, that seemed to loom ahead. In his address to the American Statistical Association, Wesley Clair Mitchell proclaimed that the war had "led to the use of statistics, not only as a record of what had happened, but also as a vital factor in planning what should be done." As he had said in his final lecture in Columbia University the previous spring, the war had shown that when the community desires to attain a great goal "then within a short period far-reaching social changes can be achieved."

"The need for scientific planning of social change," he added, "has never been greater, the chance of making those changes in an intelligent fashion has never been so good." The peace will bring new problems, he opined, but "it seems impossible" that the various countries will "attempt to solve them without utilizing the same sort of centralized directing now employed to kill their enemies abroad for the new purpose of reconstructing their own life at home."

---

[103] Hawley, "Herbert Hoover," p. 53. Also see ibid., pp. 42–54. On the continuing collaboration between Hoover, Gay, and Mitchell throughout the 1920s see Alchon, *Invisible Hand*.

But the careful empiricist and statistician also provided a caveat. Broad social planning requires "a precise comprehension of social processes" and that can be provided only by the patient research of social science. As he had written to his wife eight years earlier, Mitchell stressed that what is needed for government intervention and planning is the application of the methods of physical science and industry, particularly precise quantitative research and measurement. In contrast to the quantitative physical sciences, Mitchell told the assembled statisticians, the social sciences are "immature, speculative, filled with controversy" and class struggle. But quantitative knowledge could replace such struggle and conflict by commonly accepted precise knowledge, "objective" knowledge "amenable to mathematical formulation" and "capable of forecasting group phenomena." A statistician, Mitchell opined, is "either right or wrong," and it is easy to demonstrate which. As a result of precise knowledge of facts, Mitchell envisioned, we can achieve "intelligent experimenting and detailed planning rather than agitation and class struggle."

To achieve these vital goals none other than economists and statisticians would provide the crucial element, for we would have to be "relying more and more on trained people to plan changes for us, to follow them up, to suggest alterations."[104]

In a similar vein, the assembled economists in 1918 were regaled with the visionary presidential address of Yale economist Irving Fisher. Fisher looked forward to an economic "world reconstruction" that would provide glorious opportunities for economists to satisfy their constructive impulses. A class struggle, Fisher noted, would surely be continuing over distribution of the nation's wealth. But by devising a mechanism of "readjustment," the nation's economists could occupy an enviable role as the independent and impartial arbiters of the class

---

[104] Alchon, *Invisible Hand*, pp. 39–42; Dorfman, *Economic Mind*, vol. 3, p. 490.

struggle, these disinterested social scientists making the crucial decisions for the public good.

In short, both Mitchell and Fisher were, subtly and perhaps half-consciously, advancing the case for a postwar world in which their own allegedly impartial and scientific professions could levitate above the narrow struggles of classes for the social product, and thus emerge as a commonly accepted, "objective" new ruling class, a twentieth-century version of the philosopher-kings.

It might not be amiss to see how these social scientists, prominent in their own fields and spokesmen in different ways for the New Era of the 1920s, fared in their disquisitions and guidance for the society and the economy. Irving Fisher, as we have seen, wrote several works celebrating the alleged success of prohibition, and insisted even after 1929, that since the price level had been kept stable, there could be no depression or stock market crash. For his part, Mitchell culminated a decade of snug alliance with Herbert Hoover by directing, along with Gay and the National Bureau, a massive and hastily written work on the American economy. Published in 1929 on the accession of Hoover to the presidency, with all the resources of scientific and quantitative economics and statistics brought to bear, there is not so much as a hint in *Recent Economic Changes in the United States* that there might be a crash and depression in the offing.

The *Recent Economic Changes* study was originated and organized by Herbert Hoover, and it was Hoover who secured the financing from the Carnegie Corporation. The object was to celebrate the years of prosperity presumably produced by Secretary of Commerce Hoover's corporatist planning and to find out how the possibly future President Hoover could maintain that prosperity by absorbing its lessons and making them a permanent part of the American political structure. The volume duly declared that to maintain the current prosperity, economists, statisticians, engineers, and enlightened managers would have to work out "a technique of balance" to be installed in the economy.

Recent Economic Changes, that monument to "scientific" and political folly, went through three quick printings and was widely publicized and warmly received on all sides.[105] Edward Eyre Hunt, Hoover's long-time aide in organizing his planning activities, was so enthusiastic that he continued celebrating the book and its paean to American prosperity throughout 1929 and 1930.[106]

It is appropriate to end our section on government and statistics by noting an unsophisticated yet perceptive cry from the heart. In 1945 the Bureau of Labor Statistics approached Congress for yet another in a long line of increases in appropriations for government statistics. In the process of questioning Dr. A. Ford Hinrichs, head of the BLS, Representative Frank B. Keefe, a conservative Republican Congressman from Oshkosh, Wisconsin, put an eternal question that has not yet been fully and satisfactorily answered:

> There is no doubt but what it would be nice to have a whole lot of statistics. I am just wondering whether we are not embarking on a program that is dangerous when we keep adding and adding and adding to this thing. . . . We have been planning and getting statistics ever

---

[105] One exception was the critical review in the *Commercial and Financial Chronicle* (May 18, 1929), which derided the impression given the reader that the capacity of the United States "for continued prosperity is well-nigh unlimited." Quoted in Davis, *World Between the Wars*, p. 144. Also on *Recent Economic Changes* and economists' opinions at the time, see ibid., pp. 136–51, 400–17; David W. Eakins, "The Development of Corporate Liberal Policy Research in the United States, 1885–1965," Ph.D. diss., doctoral dissertation University of Wisconsin, 1966, pp. 166–69, 205; and Edward Angly, comp., *Oh Yeah?* (New York: Viking Press, 1931).

[106] In 1930, Hunt published a book-length, popularizing summary, *An Audit of America*. On *Recent Economic Changes*, also see Alchon, *Invisible Hand*, pp. 129–133, 135–142, 145–151, 213.

since 1932 to try to meet a situation that was domestic in character, but were never able to even meet that question. Now we are involved in an international question. It looks to me as though we spend a tremendous amount of time with graphs and charts and statistics and planning. What my people are interested in is what is it all about? Where are we going, and where are you going?[107]

[107] *Department of Labor—FSA Appropriation Bill for 1945*. Hearings Before the Subcommittee on Appropriations. 78th Congress, 2nd Session, Part I (Washington, 1945), pp. 258f., 276f. Quoted in Rothbard, "Politics of Political Economists," p. 665. On the growth of economists and statisticians in government, especially during wartime, see also Herbert Stein, "The Washington Economics Industry," *American Economic Association Papers and Proceedings* 76 (May 1986), pp. 2–3.

Index

Ludwig von Mises Institute
518 West Magnolia Avenue
Auburn, Alabama 36832